Enhancing Self-Esteem
in the Classroom

Dr **Denis Lawrence** is a chartered educational psychologist and qualified teacher with experience in primary and secondary schools as well as university departments and colleges of education. He is now in private practice as a counsellor and educational consultant. This book is based on research he has carried out over the last two decades both in Australia and in the United Kingdom.

Enhancing Self-Esteem in the Classroom

Second edition

DENIS LAWRENCE

P·C·P
Paul Chapman
Publishing Ltd

In memory of my mother, Elizabeth

ISBN 1-85396-351-8
© Denis Lawrence 1996
First published 1996
Reprinted 2002, 2003, 2005

Paul Chapman Publishing Ltd
A SAGE Publications Company
1 Oliver's Yard
55 City Road
London EC1Y 1SP

SAGE Publications Inc
2455 Teller Road
Thousand Oaks
California 91320

SAGE Publications India Pvt. Ltd
B–42 Panchsheel Enclave
PO Box 4109
New Delhi 110 017

British Library Cataloguing in Publication data
A catalogue record for this book is available from the British Library

Typeset by Dorwyn Ltd., Rowlands Castle, Hampshire
Printed digitally and bound in Great Britain by
Biddles Limited, King's Lynn, Norfolk

Contents

Acknowledgements

There would not be sufficient space to acknowledge all those people who have been influential in my writing of this book. Room must be found, however, for some.

Above all, I remain indebted to Professor Philip Gammage of the University of Nottingham for his sustained encouragement.

The many children who took part in the interviews must of course remain anonymous but my grateful thanks go out to them.

An indirect but no less powerful influence has been the example of my three daughters, Diane, Christine and Helen, who have been a continued source of inspiration.

The typing of the manuscript has been a mammoth task and I remain grateful to Ann Congrene in the early stages and to Janet Welburn in the later stages.

I am particularly grateful to my dear wife, Anne, for her professional advice in writing up this second edition.

Finally, thanks must go to Marianne Lagrange whose quiet persuasion and foresight was largely responsible for me writing this second edition.

Preface

This book is about the relationship between self-esteem and achievement. It also demonstrates the value of helping children develop self-esteem for its own sake. Children with high self-esteem are less likely to show behavioural problems and more likely to grow into responsible adults. Research is outlined showing how teachers are in a powerful position to ensure this happens. It is shown how this can come about not only through their everyday teaching but also through adopting specific programmes.

Since the first edition the need for teachers to help children develop their self-esteem has been made even more apparent. This decade has seen society steadily become more competitive and as a result the pressures on children to succeed have become greater. This is particularly true in education where pupils these days are soon made aware of the need to acquire skills before having to enter a highly competitive job market. There is a stronger emphasis these days on the need to acquire formal qualifications. In principle there is nothing wrong with that aim. However, there is the danger of focusing too much on the learning of skills to the detriment of the education of the whole child. There is a strong argument for educating for social and emotional development as well as for education of the intellect.

When the first edition came to print there was an atmosphere of experimentation in schools. Programmes to help children develop social skills were not uncommon. Sadly, in today's political climate opportunities to continue this theme appear to have faded. Teachers have always been aware of their role in helping children learn how to develop into responsible adults but in recent times they have gradually seen the erosion of the time made available for this essential aspect of education. Teachers previously committed to this approach inevitably have become disillusioned. This has had its effect on morale and ultimately on teacher self-esteem. Add to this the countless changes and innovations in education during the current decade, many of them forced on to teachers as a result of economic circumstances rather than being based on educational priorities, and it is no surprise to find more teachers than ever under stress and with low self-esteem. In the first edition of this book attention was drawn to the relationship between the self-esteem of the teacher and the self-esteem of the pupil. Teachers with high self-esteem tend to produce children with high self-esteem. However, teachers put under stress soon develop low self-esteem. It is important therefore that teachers are protected from undue stress. Once this happens, again the self-esteem of their pupils is affected. It is of concern therefore that in today's political climate teachers often seem to be overworked, confused over their roles and anxious over their futures.

It is mainly as a result of these changes in the educational climate that this revised edition was considered to be necessary. There is now a stronger need to focus more on the self-esteem of the teacher. Accordingly this edition includes additional suggestions and strategies for teachers to help them maintain their self-esteem and cope better with the effects of possible stressful experiences. Also in this edition there are additional activities for teachers to use when planning self-esteem enhancement programmes for children.

Introduction

One of the most exciting discoveries in educational psychology in recent times has been the finding that people's levels of achievement are influenced by how they feel about themselves. A vast body of research evidence has accumulated showing a positive correlation between self-esteem and achievement, and with regard to self-esteem and school achievement in particular.

Perhaps even more exciting has been the practical implications of this research for the classroom teacher. It is clear from the research that the teacher is in a powerful position to be able to influence a student's self-esteem not only through the use of systematic activities but also through the establishment of particular caring relationships with students. The work of the humanist school of psychology has focused on certain ingredients of personality which are instrumental in the latter. There is clear evidence that relationships between teacher and students can be either conducive to the enhancement or self-esteem or conducive towards reducing self-esteem.

Whenever the teacher enters into a relationship with a student a process is set into motion which results either in the enhancement of self-esteem or in the reduction of self-esteem. Moreover, this process occurs whether the teacher is aware of it or not. Whilst some teachers may intuitively enhance the self-esteem of their students, the evidence is that all teachers might well benefit from an awareness of the principles involved in self-esteem enhancement.

Teaching is more effective when the teacher is able to combine an approach which focuses not only on the development of skills but also on the student's effective state, and on self-esteem in particular. The evidence points to the view that teachers do not have to make a decision whether to teach for skills or self-esteem enhancement – they can do both simultaneously. Indeed, the successful teacher has always combined the behavioural with the affective approach. After all, teaching has traditionally been mainly a process of human interaction.

Recent developments, however, have tended to focus on the 'non-human' aspects of the teaching process. Developments in high technology and the introduction to schools of the computer have without doubt greatly extended the repertoire of the teacher to the benefit of many children. The danger is that there may be a temptation to regard this and other technological advances as substitutes for the teacher. A greater danger is perhaps the present emphasis on direct instruction.

In a longitudinal study looking at 4-year-olds in three types of education, Schweinhart *et al.* (1986) made the alarming discovery that children who had had Direct Instruction (DISTAR) did not have as positive a self-image at ages 5, 8 and 15 as did others in the study who did not receive Direct Instruction. A third of the children in this study carried out their own preschool programme work, a third received Distar and a third 'ordinary' nursery provision. The two-thirds that had not received Direct Instruction generally were seen to be more cooperative, more highly motivated with regard to higher education and less likely to be delinquent.

Whatever the merits or demerits of this piece of research, it is a timely reminder that education is not just about learning cognitive skills. It is also about helping children to learn about themselves, to be able to live peaceably with themselves and with others, and to help them develop into competent, mature, self-motivated adults. Although Direct Instruction continues to emphasize the role of the teacher, the effective interaction between teacher and child is minimized, and so also is the opportunity for children to develop personal skills. There can be no substitute for the enthusiasm, warmth and spontaneity of the personal encounter.

Gammage (1986) focuses on this issue when criticizing a DES circular in Britain on teacher training. There seems to be an official view that teachers should concentrate more on the acquisition of knowledge, reminiscent of 'back to basics' philosophy often expressed in the 1960s, and less on the process of teaching. In the words of Gammage, '*how* teachers teach is as important an issue as *what* they teach', but the DFEE seems to be caught up with the behaviourist philosophy with its concentration on the observable behaviour to the exclusion of affective factors.

If the message is so clear why are so many teachers apparently unaware of the importance of teaching for self-esteem enhancement? One reason for this could be that the researchers have not easily communicated their findings, and have tended to confuse issues with a lack of consensus on substantive definitions. For instance, English and English (1958) identify over a thousand different combinations and uses of the terms in the self-concept area with the same terms often used to mean different things and again different terms such as *self-esteem, self-concept, self-image* often used to mean the same thing. It is not surprising then if some teachers have been confused when the researchers themselves appear to be unable to define their terms properly. Fortunately this has all begun to come together to the satisfaction of most workers in the self-concept area and the definitions of Argyle (1970) are now generally accepted. This aspect is outlined in the first chapter when the development of self-esteem is also discussed.

A second possible reason why teachers have given little prominence to self-esteem enhancement could be the relative absence of guidelines on how to set about the task. Admittedly most teachers are aware of the need to provide positive reinforcements and may be familiar with self-esteem enhancement activities such as those suggested by Canfield and Wells (1976), but often they are left with the feeling of something missing. It is suggested that this missing link is their own part in the process, that is, the qualities of personality and the combination skills of the teacher. This link is vital.

Burns (1979b), for instance, draws attention to the way in which the teacher's self-esteem influences the child's self-esteem. Rogers (1951) identifies the skills of communication which can be learned, and which teachers need to learn to become more effective. Interestingly, the same skills are those which are related to the development of the self-concept and also associated with successful counselling. This topic will be pursued further, not only in connection with the teacher's personality but also in connection with communication skills important in the counselling programmes outlined in Chapter 5.

The main purpose of this book, therefore, is to help teachers appreciate how they can influence self-esteem of students in the classroom and also to give practical guidelines on how to do this.

Although the ideas in this book focus mainly on self-esteem and its relationship to achievement the clear corollary is that self-esteem enhancement is a worthwhile teaching aim in its own right. After all, education means more than the learning of academic skills. If we can help children to understand themselves better and to feel more confident about themselves then they are going to be in a stronger position to be able to cope with the inevitable stresses of life and to be better citizens. Teachers are in an ideal role to be able to influence this development. Self-esteem enhancement contributes positively towards both academic achievement and towards personal and social development. The book is aimed at both primary and secondary teachers as the principles and practices apply from the primary stage to the secondary stage.

Chapter 1 clarifies the terms used and outlines the development of self-esteem.

Chapter 2 looks at the question of assessing self-esteem and presents a standardized questionnaire for use by teacher.

Chapter 3 considers self-esteem enhancement as a framework to all teaching, and focuses on the quality of the student–teacher relationship.

Chapter 4 outlines games and activities which have been used successfully to enhance self-esteem amongst students with low self-esteem.

Chapter 5 sets out a counselling programme which can be used either by teachers or other workers with low self-esteem students.

Chapter 6 considers the role of self-esteem in the management of behavioural difficulties.

Chapter 7 looks at self-esteem enhancement as part of a remedial reading programme.

Chapter 8 discusses the importance of the teacher's own self-esteem, and suggests ways of maintaining high self-esteem.

Finally, the Appendix discusses the author's research findings on which the counselling programmes in this book are based.

Chapter 1

What is self-esteem?

Clarifying the terminology

What is self-esteem? We all have our own idea of what we mean by the term, but in any discussion of self-esteem amongst a group of teachers there are likely to be several different definitions. The chances are that amongst these definitions the words *self-concept, ideal self* and *self-image* will appear.

The fact is that the literature until fairly recently has tended to use many terms like these to mean the same thing. It is no wonder teachers therefore have been confused and as a result have tended to dismiss the concept as yet another of those ambiguous terms so often found in discussions of education. Fortunately, the concept has gradually been more clearly defined thanks to the work of people like Argyle in Britain and Rogers in the USA.

Self-concept

First, the term *self-concept* is best defined as the sum total of an individual's mental and physical characteristics and his/her evaluation of them. As such it has three aspects: the cognitive (thinking); the affective (feeling); and the behavioural (action). In practice, and from the teacher's point of view, it is useful to consider this self-concept as developing in three areas – self-image, ideal self and self-esteem. Self-esteem, of course, is the focus of this book. To understand the concept of self-esteem, however, it is necessary to define self-image and ideal self. Self-concept is the umbrella term under which the other three develop.

The self-concept is the individual's awareness of his/her own self. It is an awareness of one's own identity. The complexity of the nature of the 'self' has occupied the thinking of philosophers for centuries and was not considered to be a proper topic for psychology until James (1890) resurrected the concept from the realms of philosophy. As with the philosophers of his day, James wrestled with the objective and subjective nature of the 'self' – and 'me' and the 'I' – and eventually concluded that it was perfectly reasonable for the psychologist to study the 'self' as an objective phenomenon. He envisaged the infant developing from 'one big blooming buzzing confusion' to the eventual adult state of self-consciousness. The process of development throughout life can be considered, therefore, as a process of becoming more and more aware of one's own characteristics and consequent feelings about them. We see the *self-concept* as an umbrella term (see Figure 1.1) because subsumed beneath the 'self' there are three aspects: self-image (what the person is); ideal self (what the person would like to be); and self-esteem (what the person feels about the discrepancy between what he/she is and what he/she would like to be).

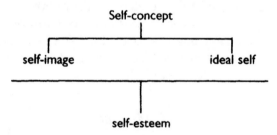

Figure 1.1   Self-concept as an umbrella term

To understand the umbrella nature of the term readers might like to ask themselves the question, 'Who am I?', several times. When first asked the answer is likely to be name and perhaps sex. When asked a second time the person's job or occupation may be given. The self-image is being revealed so far. Further questioning will lead to the need to reveal more of the person and, in so doing, the ideal self and the self-esteem. For example,

'I am a confident person' (self-esteem); 'I would like to be able to play cricket' (ideal self).

Each of the three aspects of self-concept will be considered in turn. Underpinning this theoretical account of the development of self-concept will be the notion that it is the child's *interpretation* of the life experience which determines self-esteem levels. This is known as the phenomenological approach and owes its origin mainly to the work of Rogers (1951). It attempts to understand a person through empathy with that person and is based on the premiss that it is not the events which determine emotions but rather the person's interpretation of the events. To be able to understand the other person requires therefore an ability to empathize.

Self-image

Self-image is the individual's awareness of his/her mental and physical characteristics. It begins in the family with parents giving the child an image of him/herself of being loved or not loved, of being clever or stupid, and so forth, by their non-verbal as well as verbal communication. This process becomes less passive as the child him/herself begins to initiate further personal characteristics. The advent of school brings other experiences for the first time and soon the child is learning that he/she is popular or not popular with other children. He/she learns that school work is easily accomplished or otherwise. A host of mental and physical characteristics are learned according to how rich and varied school life becomes. In fact one could say that the more experiences one has, the richer is the self-image.

The earliest impressions of self-image are mainly concepts of *body-image*. The child soon learns that he/she is separate from the surrounding environment. This is sometimes seen amusingly in the young baby who bites its foot only to discover with pain that the foot belongs to itself. Development throughout infancy is largely a process of this further awareness of body as the senses develop. The image becomes more precise and accurate with increasing maturity so that by adolescence the individual is normally fully aware not only of body shape and size but also of his/her attractiveness in relation to peers.

Sex-role identity also begins at an early age, probably at birth, as parents and others begin their stereotyping and classifying of the child into one sex or the other.

With cognitive development more refined physical and mental skills become possible, including reading and sporting pursuits. These are usually predominant in most schools so that the child soon forms an awareness of his/her capabilities in these areas.

This process of development of the self-image has been referred to as the 'looking-glass theory of self' (Cooley, 1902) as most certainly the individual is forming his/her self-image as he/she receives feedback from others. However, the process is not wholly a matter of 'bouncing *off* the environment' but also one of 'reflecting *on* the environment' as cognitive abilities make is possible for individuals to reflect on their experiences and interpret them.

Self-image is our starting point for an understanding of self-esteem.

Ideal self

Side by side with the development of self-image the child is learning that there are ideal characteristics he/she should possess – that there are ideal standards of behaviour and also particular skills which are valued. For example, adults place value on being clean and tidy, and 'being clever' is important. As with self-image the process begins in the family and continues on entry to school. The child is becoming aware of the mores of the society. Body-image, again, is one of the earliest impressions of the ideal self as parents comment on the shape and size of their child. Soon the child is comparing him/herself with others and eventually with peers. Peer comparisons are particularly powerful at adolescence. The influence of the media also becomes a significant factor at this time with various advertising and show-business personalities providing models of aspiration.

With maturity a person's total experiences are able to be evaluated more realistically although it is doubtful whether a person ever becomes sufficiently mature to be completely uninfluenced. Our early experiences may continue to influence our present behaviour to some extent although we all have the potential for becoming self-determinate. The schoolchild is most likely to be at the stages of accepting these ideal images from the significant people around him/her and of striving to a greater or lesser degree to attain them.

Self-esteem

Self-esteem is the individual's *evaluation* of the discrepancy between self-image and ideal self. It is an affective process and is a measure of the extent to which the individual cares about this discrepancy. From the discussion on the development of self-image and ideal self it can be appreciated that the discrepancy between the two is inevitable and so can be regarded as a normal phenomenon.

Indeed, there is evidence from clinical work that without this discrepancy – without levels of aspiration – individuals can become apathetic and poorly adjusted. Just as in physiology the nerve impulse is always active so it seems that the psyche also needs to be active. It is a mistake to think that the ideal state is one of total relaxation. Whilst this may be desirable for a short while, in the long run it can produce neurotic behaviour. For the person to be striving is therefore a normal state.

What is not so normal is that the individual should worry and become distressed over the discrepancy. Clearly, this is going to depend in early childhood on how the significant people in the child's life react to him/her. For instance, if the parent is overanxious about the child's development this will soon be communicated and the child, too, will also become overanxious about it. He/she begins first by trying to fulfil the parental expectations but if he/she is not able to meet them begins to feel guilty.

It is interesting that the young child is so trusting in the adults that he/she does not consider that they could be wrong or misguided. When a child fails to live up to parental expectations he/she blames him/herself at first, feeling unworthy of their love. Moreover, this failure in a particular area generalizes so that he/she would not just feel a failure say in reading attainment, but will feel a failure as a person generally. The child is not able to compartmentalize his/her life as can the adult. If we adults cannot play chess, for instance, we avoid the chess club. If the child fails in, say, reading, he/she cannot avoid the situation.

Indeed, the subject of reading is probably the most important skill he/she will learn in the primary school and normally will come into contact with reading every day of school life. It is not surprising therefore that the child who fails in reading over a lengthy period should be seen to have developed low self-esteem, the end product of feeling guilt about his/her failure. The child then lacks confidence in him/herself.

It can be appreciated from the foregoing description of the development of self-concept that teachers are in a very strong position to be able to influence self-esteem. It should be pointed out perhaps at this juncture that not all children who fail in school work will have low self-esteem. Those parents, and sometimes those teachers, who put no pressure at all on the child to achieve will not of course be worrying the child over his/her failure. But at the same time, without some demands being made on the child he/she will not likely be achieving.

The rule is: unrealistic demands may result in low self-esteem, but no demands at all may result in no achievement. Clearly, there must be an optimum amount of pressure – just enough to cause the child to care but not too much so that he/she becomes distressed. The secret is to be aware of the child's present level of functioning so that our demands to extend this level will be realistic. In the area of language development, for instance, we should not normally expect our child to be able to use a long, complex sentence structure until his/her span of attention and memory-span have developed sufficiently to be able to retain it. It can be appreciated at once that the child's present level of functioning in any area is likely to depend on a complex inter-relatedness of many factors. Only an intimate knowledge of the child will give us this information.

In summary, it is not failure to achieve which produces low self-esteem, it is the way the significant people in the child's life react to the failure. Indeed, it could be argued that failure is an inevitable part of life. There is always someone cleverer or more skilful than ourselves. This must be accepted if we are to help children develop happily without straining always to be on top. Eventually, of course, children become aware of their own level of achievement and realize that they are not performing as well as others around them. Then they can develop low self-esteem irrespective of the opinions of others; they have set their own standards. It is probably true to say, however, that the primary schoolchild is still likely to be 'internalizing' his/her ideal self from the significant people around him/her. These people of course can include peers as well as teachers and family.

How self-esteem operates

The child with high self-esteem is likely to be confident in social situations and in tackling school work. He/she will have retained a natural curiosity for learning and will be eager and enthusiastic when presented with a new challenge.

The child with low self-esteem, in contrast, will lack confidence in his/her ability to succeed. Consequently, he/she may try to avoid situations which he/she sees as potentially personally humiliating. In the words of the famous philosopher and psychologist William James (1890), 'With no attempt there can be no failure; with no failure no humiliation'. This explains why some students prefer to do nothing even though knowing they are likely to incur the teacher's displeasure. To be punished and perhaps be seen as something of a hero by their peers is better than to be seen to be foolish.

Avoidance and compensation

Depending on whether the child is by temperament inclined to extroversion or introversion, he/she will meet the situation with avoidance or an attempt to compensate. If inclined to extroversion he/she is more likely to compensate and fight back at the source of the frustration. So we can have the child who is arrogant and boastful on the surface and so giving an impression of anything but low self-esteem. At its extreme this would be the classical 'inferiority complex' as coined by Jung (1923). On the other hand, if introverted by temperament, the child is more likely to withdraw and demonstrate the shy, timid behaviour which common sense tells us immediately is an indication of low self-esteem.

In both cases the child is avoiding the feeling of failure. Clearly, if he/she avoids work the teacher is going to be alerted, but more often than not, this then takes the form of exhorting the child to 'get down and do some work' or even a mental note that 'this child is lazy'. It can be appreciated, however, that the child is merely communicating that he/she would rather risk the wrath of the teacher than suffer the feeling of humiliation which he/she sees as the inevitable consequence of tackling new work.

The question is: Why is humiliation so terrible and to be avoided at all costs? To answer this question we turn to the humanistic psychologists, of whom the best known, perhaps, is Carl Rogers (1961). Carl Rogers has drawn our attention to the prime need in our culture for self-regard. In a society where generally people no longer starve, and where primitive drives are easily expressed, it seems that our most important need is to preserve self-esteem. Whether this is innate or learned does not matter. We all need to be liked and to be valued. When we cannot fulfil this need easily we tend to identify this with material things which we know will be admired and so set out to possess as large a car or as large a house as we can. Or, we may divert this need into our children, not just by basking in their achievement, but sometimes misguidedly living out our own lives through them.

Motivation

A second phenomenon of the self-concept is that it is a 'motivator'. We all tend to behave in ways which fit in with our perception of ourselves. Indeed, we can feel decidedly insecure when we are expected to behave in a manner which we might regard as 'not me'. One example of this would be the shy, low self-esteem child who is suddenly called upon to read the address at the school assembly in front of perhaps 400 others. Consider also the student teacher facing a class for the first time. Both are going to feel very anxious indeed.

At a less dramatic level, but none the less important, is the retarded reader who daydreams during the school library sessions. He/she does not see reading as relevant to his/her self-concept. Reading is for the 'clever ones'. Even though the child may comply with the teacher's demand to read he/she would just 'go through the motions' of reading without really being highly motivated. This would mean, of course, that any learning which did take place would not be retained in the long term.

This child can baffle the teacher as he/she seems to learn in the short term. In addition he/she seems to possess all the skills necessary to make progress. Often, these children score well in intelligence tests and show no perceptual difficulties, neither are they showing overt signs of emotional disturbance. However, without attention to their low self-esteem they are not likely to make long-term progress.

Resistance

A third important feature of self-concept is that it tends to be resistant to change. This means that we cannot reasonably expect our retarded reader suddenly to see him/herself as a potentially good reader, even with therapeutic intervention. It can be quite threatening for a retarded child to be informed that he/she will soon be 'clever' and be able to read. It needs to be a gradual process.

It seems that it is just 'human nature' to want to maintain self-consistency. It is quite startling to meet people with the most severe of handicaps desperately clinging to their handicaps in the face of a possible change. We need to know who we are and the familiar is safer than the unfamiliar even if known to be inadequate. The hearing-impaired person may resist at first an operation which can restore the hearing merely because of the risk to self-concept. This is not meant to suggest he/she would not eventually go through with the operation but it is not an easy decision to make when it also means changing the self-concept.

The low self-esteem person is even more resistant to change as it means taking risks which he/she cannot easily do in the sense of either learning new skills or being a different person. Any remedial approach to the child with a learning difficulty should therefore take this factor into account.

The self-esteem hierarchy

The question often posed is 'Can we have low self-esteem in one situation and high self-esteem in another?' It is only asked by those who have not understood the hierarchical nature of self-esteem (Shavelson *et al.*, 1976).

Self-esteem as defined so far refers to a 'global self-esteem' – an individual's overall feeling of self-worth. This is relatively stable and consistent over time. In addition to this overall, or global, self-esteem we can have feelings of worth or unworthiness in specific situations. Accordingly we may feel inadequate (low self-esteem) with regard to mathematics or tennis playing. However, they do not affect our overall feeling of self-worth as we can escape their influences by avoiding those situations. If, of course, we cannot avoid them and regularly participate in these activities which make us feel inadequate they may eventually affect our overall self-esteem. Also if we continue to fail in areas which are valued by the significant people in our lives then our overall self-esteem is affected. It is worth reflecting on how children cannot escape school subjects which is why failure in school so easily generalizes to the global self-esteem.

It is important to appreciate this hierarchy of self-esteem as confusion often arises when people make statements such as 'Girls have lower self-esteem than boys'. This is not borne out by the research if we are referring to global self-esteem (Marsh *et al.*, 1984), but it is true when referring to mathematics and science. Even here we must be careful to distinguish between statistical significance and practical significance. The research mentioned refers to statistical significance but the differences *within* the sexes are greater so that, practically, we can say there are no real differences between the sexes. Figure 1.2 illustrates the self-esteem hierarchy (for a more detailed account, see Shavelson and Bolus, 1982).

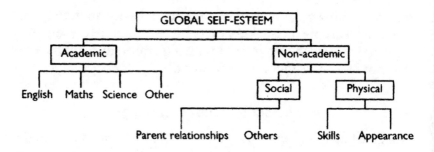

Figure 1.2 The self-esteem hierarchy

In summary, self-esteem develops as a result of interpersonal relationships within the family which gradually give precedence to school influences and to the influences of the larger society in which the individual chooses to live and to work. These extraneous influences lose their potency to the extent to which the individual becomes self-determinate. For the student of school age, however, self-esteem continues to be affected mainly by the significant people in the life of the student, usually parents, teachers and peers.

The evidence for self-esteem enhancement

The need to maintain children's self-esteem is self-evident and most teachers are well aware of the importance of the value attached to helping children feel good about themselves. On commonsense grounds one would expect children with high self-esteem to do better in class than children with low self-esteem. And this is supported by the research which consistently shows a positive correlation between children's self-esteem and their levels of attainment. The correlational studies usually reveal a figure around 0.6, which indicates that other factors are also relevant in whether children achieve or not. Obviously, ability is an essential factor in the achievement equation. However, it is clear from the research that children will not use their full ability if their self-esteem is low. This is well documented in research carried out by the author and also in other published research (Purkey, 1970; West *et al.*, 1980; Burns, 1982).

It is over 25 years since the first of a long series of experiments was begun by the author in Somerset, England, into the enhancement of children's self-esteem. The original experiments concluded that teachers were able to enhance children's self-esteem over a six-month period through a systematic programme of counselling. This is discussed in more detail in Appendix 1. Following these experiments it was hypothesized that the results were a function of the quality of the relationships established and not necessarily dependent on either the academic or professional qualifications of the author. If this were the case it should be possible for non-professionals to obtain the same results. A further series of experiments were then conducted using people to do the counselling who were not professionally trained. They were simply briefed on self-concept theory as outlined above and shown how to organize the sessions.

They were seen to obtain the same results as a professional psychologist. It was becoming clear that the essential ingredient in the process was the communication skills of the counsellor, as discussed in Chapter 5. The conclusion from these experiments was not that teachers or psychologists were unsuited to this task. Indeed, on commonsense grounds, with their training and knowledge of children, they should be even more skilled than non-professionals. The significant conclusion was that no matter what the professional qualifications of the counsellor, they would not be effective unless they also possessed the qualities of personality which the research in counselling shows to be essential. Brief details of these experiments are given in the Appendix.

The results of the above experiments were later translated into workshops for teachers. Sad to relate, however, very few schools appeared to put them into practice. This is not the place to discuss fully the reasons for this but as has been the case so often in education, lack of money was one of the reasons. The author was subsequently invited by the Western Australian Government Department of Education to conduct self-esteem workshops throughout that state and over 200 schools were eventually served. Despite the dismal circumstance regarding financing education in the UK it is encouraging to note that, today, many schools in the UK are at last beginning to appreciate the significance of a self-esteem programme. It is to be hoped that this trend will continue.

The research evidence does not point only to the correlation between self-esteem and academic achievement. There is also evidence of a correlation between self-esteem and children's behaviour. It seems that children with high self-esteem are more likely to get on better with others and so have fewer behaviour problems. In the experiments reported, teachers regularly mentioned a reduction in behavioural difficulties amongst those who had been counselled, although this was not the main object of the programme. The self-esteem enhancement programme was more modest in its aims, merely trying to help children change their attitudes towards themselves. Not all children who have low self-esteem have behavioural difficulties. The fact that the self-esteem experiments did not specifically aim to reduce behavioural difficulties is important in highlighting the similarities and differences between a self-esteem programme and one aimed to help children who do show behavioural difficulties. The latter are discussed in more detail in Chapter 6. However, it should be mentioned that research concludes that when a teacher is faced with children showing behavioural difficulties, no matter what sanctions or disciplinary measures the teacher may decide to use, the manner in which they are used is crucial with regard to the child's self-esteem. Also, research concludes that self-esteem enhancement need not by any means be inconsistent with good discipline in the classroom. Children in any context who know where the boundaries to their behaviour lie and how far they can go generally feel more secure and are usually of higher self-esteem. The famous research of Stanley Coopersmith (1967) into behaviour and attitudes, although conducted over 25 years ago, is just as valid today.

Self-esteem enhancement does not mean always that focus has to be on helping children feel good about themselves. Some children are so immature that they are still relatively unconscious of themselves and often the best way to help them is to try to help them become more aware of their behaviour. Ask these children why they behaved in a particular way and they usually answer 'I don't know'. This can infuriate the adult asking the question but it is generally the case that they genuinely do not know. For them any programme of self-esteem enhancement should be shelved until they are aware of a self to be enhanced!

Perhaps one of the most startling of research findings is the conclusion that there is a correlation between children's self-esteem and teacher self-esteem. Children of high self-esteem who are in regular contact with teachers of low self-esteem will gradually themselves develop low self-esteem, with associated low attainment levels. On a more positive note, the converse can also occur, with low self-esteem children raising their self-esteem through regular contact with high self-esteem teachers (Burns, 1982).

It is clear from all the research that teachers are in a powerful position to influence children's self-esteem and in turn influence their achievements and behaviour. Perhaps most teachers are already aware of this, and probably already enhance children's self-esteem intuitively. However, a knowledge of the research, together with familiarity with self-concept theory, would provide teachers with a proper rationale so that they are in a position to know how to go about enhancing self-esteem systematically.

The research would suggest that teachers can enhance self-esteem in three ways:

1. Through a systematic programme of group activities lasting usually a term. These are described in Chapter 4.
2. Through individual counselling, although the phrase 'listening to children' might be preferred to describe this procedure. This is discussed in Chapter 5.
3. Through providing a positive ethos in the classroom. This is probably the most usual way in which teachers influence children's self-esteem. This is the method which is more likely to be done on an intuitive basis. The self-esteem and communication skills of the teacher are the significant factors in this process, as discussed in Chapter 3. Teachers can either reduce or enhance children's self-esteem according to how they manage the general ethos of the classroom.

Self-esteem enhancement does not have to take the form of a systematic programme. The opinion has been expressed in some quarters that teachers do not always have time for self-esteem enhancement. This view is based on a false premiss of what self-esteem enhancement is about. All teaching should be carried out within a generally self-esteem enhancing framework.

Further reading

Dewhurst, D. (1991) Should teachers enhance their pupils' self-esteem? *Journal of Moral Education* Vol. 20, no. 1, pp. 3–11.
Greenhalgh, P. (1994) *Emotional Growth & Learning*. Routledge, London.
Marston, A.R. (1986) Dealing with low self-confidence. *Educational Research*, Vol. 10, pp. 134–138.
Stevens, R. (1995) *Understanding the Self*. Sage, London.

Chapter 2

Assessing self-esteem

In theory it should be a simple matter to identify those with low self-esteem. Having defined self-esteem as 'the individual's affective evaluation of the discrepancy between self-image and ideal self', surely, it might be argued, all that is required is to devise a series of questions which ask the individual how he/she feels about this discrepancy.

The fact is that there are very few methods of assessing self-esteem which can be considered to be sufficiently reliable and valid for the purpose of practical usage in the classroom. One reason for this is the history of the research into self-concept. As there have been so many different theories of personality over the years inevitably there have been many different definitions of self-esteem and so as a result many different kinds of assessment procedures (Wylie, 1974). In a book such as this which aims to be a practical handbook a review of the methodology would be inappropriate. It is appropriate, however, that teachers are aware of some of the difficulties involved in accurately assessing self-esteem.

The checklist

The teacher with an acquaintance with self-concept theory as outlined in Chapter 1 will be on the lookout for the student who lacks confidence, who seems apathetic, who seems unable to take risks, and the like. Indeed, the following checklist might be used to assess low self-esteem:

- Does he/she make self-disparaging remarks?

- Is he/she boastful?
- Is he/she hesitant and timid in new situations?
- Does he/she make excuses to avoid situations which may be stressful?
- Is he/she continually asking for help and/or reassurance?
- Is he/she continually asking if he/she is liked or is popular?
- Does he/she hang back and remain on the fringe of a group?
- Is he/she apathetic in a learning situation?
- Does he/she daydream a lot?
- Does he/she avoid work even though risking your displeasure?
- Does he/she tend to blame others for his/her failures?
- Is he/she reluctant to assume responsibilities?

Even where the teacher feels the student shows many of these characteristics the problem is, however, that the feelings of low self-esteem are merely being *inferred*. They cannot be observed directly.

One way of getting around the problem of inferring the feelings of low self-esteem might seem to be the questionnaire. By asking the student directly how he/she feels should be a more reliable way of assessing self-esteem. Unfortunately this method is also subject to certain difficulties of reliability. It is obvious that people can fake their responses and also may be subject to 'social desirability' response, that is, they will tend to reply in a socially accepted way. Moreover, some students may not be able to describe their feelings accurately.

From the preceding arguments it can be appreciated that methods of assessment of self-esteem are not going to be 100 per cent reliable. However, in our present state of knowledge the checklist method is probably the simplest to use and is useful as long as we remember its limitations.

The 'Lawseq' questionnaires

The questionnaire is also useful provided that the standardization has been thorough and that good rapport is established between teacher and students before it is administered. Teachers may find the ones devised by me particularly useful owing to their brevity. Full details of their standardization are given in Lawrence (1982; 1983) but the actual questionnaires are shown

PRIMARY VERSION

	Yes	No	Don't know

1. Do you think that your parents usually like to hear about your ideas?
2. Do you often feel lonely at school?
3. Do other children often break friends or fall out with you?
4. Do you like team games?
5. Do you think that other children often say nasty things about you?
6. When you have to say things in front of teachers, do you usually feel shy?
7. Do you like writing stories or doing creative writing?
8. Do you often feel sad because you have nobody to play with at school?
9. Are you good at mathematics?
10. Are there lots of things about yourself you would like to change?
11. When you have to say things in front of other children, do you usually feel foolish?
12. Do you find it difficult to do things like woodwork or knitting?
13. When you want to tell a teacher something do you usually feel foolish?
14. Do you often have to find new friends because your old friends are playing with somebody else?
15. Do you usually feel foolish when you talk to your parents?
16. Do other people often think that you tell lies?

KEY:
Score +2 for all numbers answering 'no' *except* for question 1. Score +2 for question 1 answering 'yes'. 4, 7, 9, 12 do not count.

Score +1 for all answers 'don't know'.

Figure 2.1 Lawseq pupil questionnaire

SECONDARY SCHOOL VERSION

		Yes	No	Don't know

1. Do you think that your parents usually like to hear about your ideas?
2. Do you often feel lonely at school?
3. Do other students often get fed up with you and stop being friends with you?
4. Do you like outdoor games?
5. Do you think that other students often dislike you?
6. When you have to say things in front of teachers, do you usually feel shy?
7. Do you like writing stories or doing creative writing?
8. Do you often feel sad because you have nobody to talk to at school?
9. Are you good at mathematics?
10. Are there lots of things about yourself you would like to change?
11. When you have to say things in front of other students, do you usually feel foolish?
12. Do you find it difficult to do things like woodwork or knitting?
13. When you want to tell a teacher something do you usually feel foolish?
14. Do you often have to find new friends because your old friends prefer others to you?
15. Do you usually feel foolish when you talk to your parents?
16. Do other people often think that you tell lies?

KEY:
Score +2 for all numbers answering 'no' *except* for question 1. Score +2 for question 1 answering 'yes'. 4, 7, 9, 12 do not count.

Score +1 for all answers 'don't know'.

© 1996 Denis Lawrence

Figure 2.2   Lawseq student questionnaire

with both the primary (Figure 2.1) and secondary school (Figure 2.2) versions.

The questionnaires have been standardized on both an English and an Australian population with the following norms:

Primary version   Mean = 19 SD = 4
Secondary school version   Mean = 18 SD = 4

The relevant questionnaire provides a useful screening device for the busy teacher new to a class and who would like to make a quick assessment. It also provides the teacher with a handy research tool for those who may be embarking on a self-esteem enhancement programme and require a 'before' and 'after' measure.

Perhaps the most reliable method of assessing self-esteem is to find time to get to know a student personally, which of course is not always possible. The 'Lawseq', therefore, would seem to be the teacher's favoured method to date.

Other methods of assessment

Bearing in mind some of the major difficulties of assessment referred to earlier, there are other methods of assessment which the teacher may wish to consider in particular circumstances.

Rating scales

Rating scales are useful where the teacher may be interested in assessing perhaps only one or two aspects of self-esteem, for example, reluctance to attempt a new task. A 3- or 5-point scale could be used and the pupil rated accordingly:

'Afraid to attempt a new task'
Always – Sometimes – Never

Adjectival discrepancies

Adjectival discrepancies constitute a method of assessing the relationship between two different attitudes and were used by James (1890) who devised the formula:

Self-esteem = Success ÷ Pretentions

In the modern form it has been used by presenting a list of predetermined adjectives. The person is asked to go through the list; the first time a tick is placed against those which *apply* and the second time a tick is placed next to those which the person *would like to apply*. The total discrepancy between the two scores is then the measure of self-esteem.

Semantic differential

Semantic differential is a variation of the adjectival discrepancy method but this time each adjective is paired with its opposite, for example, *Easy–Difficult*. Different adjectives can be selected according to the teacher's interest. Originally devised by Osgood *et al.* (1957) it is often used as a personality trait or attitude measure outside the field of self-concept. Its main advantage is that it clarifies the adjective when the opposite is presented at the same time.

Q-sort

Q-sort is a method that has been used extensively by Rogers in connection mainly with client-centred counselling. It involves the sorting into different piles of a series of cards each containing a statement about the self; for example, 'I am always happy'.

The cards are ranked in order of how the person sees him/herself. A second ranking is made with the person considering how he/she would like to be. A prescribed set of 100 cards devised by Butler and Haigh (1954) is probably the one most frequently used.

Other variations of the method have included a list made up from the person's own past experiences and used mainly in clinical work. The literature to date lists around 22 different sets of cards which have been devised for various kinds of experiments. A big disadvantage in its use with children in the classroom is its time-consuming nature.

Projective technique

Projective techniques have been used extensively in clinical work with the best known probably being the Rorschach (inkblot test). The person is asked to say what picture he/she sees in the inkblot and the experimenter then interprets the response. Clearly, some training is necessary for the operation of this method. It has many critics in view of its subjective nature.

However, a more useful modern form of the method for use with children is the 'draw a person' test developed by Machover (1949). The child is simply asked to 'draw a person and then to include him/herself in the drawing'. The aim is to interpret the size and quality of the figures drawn in relation to the figure drawn to represent the child. Obviously, this is open to many criticisms of reliability and validity, but it is an interesting method with possibilities.

A variation of the projective technique is the 'sentence completions' test, when the person is asked to complete a partial sentence, for example, 'I feel shy when . . .'

The main difficulty with all these projective techniques is the problem of devising a standardized scoring procedure. They reveal information of a more general nature than just self-esteem and do not easily lend themselves to use in the classroom.

Other questionnaires

Questionnaire methods are certainly the easiest to use with pupils in the classroom and are probably the most frequently used as a result. In addition to the 'Lawseq' already mentioned, there are several others which have been well standardized. Unfortunately most of them have been standardized on populations outside the UK. Amongst those worth considering are the Coopersmith (1967) and the Piers–Harris (1969).

From this very brief survey of some of the most popular methods of assessing self-esteem it can be appreciated that the whole area of assessment of self-esteem is still very much in its infancy. As discussed at the beginning of this chapter, the problems are mainly of validity and reliability of the methods themselves. However, for the teacher who may wish to pursue this topic further, perhaps from the point of view of a research project, the following are recommended as reference:

1. Wells, L. and Marwell, G. (1976) *Self-Esteem: Its Conceptualisation and Measurement*, Sage, London.

2. Burns, R.B. (1979) *The Self-Concept: Theory, Measurement, Development, and Behaviour,* Longman, London.

Finally, it should be emphasized that people can manifest radically different behaviour as a response to their low self-esteem. As mentioned in Chapter 1, people can be found to lie somewhere along the continuum of introversion/extroversion. It seems to be the case that those with problems tend to be at the extremes of this continuum so it is possible to group broadly the low self-esteem students into those whose reaction is introverted and those whose reaction to low self-esteem is more extroverted.

From the work of Eysenck (1980) it seems that people react to frustration in terms of their basic personality type so that the introverted student will appear relatively apathetic whereas the extroverted student will appear perhaps as boastful and arrogant. In the latter case it is likely to be a compensation for feelings of inferiority. It is so easy to mistake this behaviour for high self-esteem.

Further reading

Lawrence, D. (1982) Development of a self-esteem questionnaire. *British Journal of Education/Psychology,* Vol. 51.

Rosenburg, M. *et al.* (1995) Global self-esteem, specific self-esteem: different concepts, different outcomes. *American Sociological Review,* Vol. 60, Feb.

Stalman, D. (1993) Self-assessment, self-esteem, and self-acceptance. *Journal of Moral Education,* Vol. 22, no. 1.

Wells, L. and Marwell, G. (1982) *Self-esteem: Its Conceptualisation and Its Measurement.* Sage Publications, London.

Chapter 3

Enhancing self-esteem while teaching

The experiments outlined in Appendix 1 and also referred to on pp 11–12, show how it is possible to enhance self-esteem and also increase academic achievement through either counselling or drama. It can be appreciated, however, from the discussion on the development of self-concept that the teacher should be in a position to influence self-esteem in other ways in addition to the methods outlined in the experiments. There is evidence that teaching is more effective where the teacher can establish close relationships.

The work of Argyle (1970) draws attention to the factors involved in attitude change and in some ways self-esteem can be likened to an attitude towards oneself. Argyle shows how attitudes are more easily influenced when the person who sets out to change attitudes has status and is capable of making a warm relationship with the subject. Teachers generally have status, at least in the eyes of their pupils, but it is the warm relationship which is sometimes missing. However, those teachers who have status and do have a warm relationship with their pupils are more likely to affect the self-esteem level of their pupils.

Desirable counselling qualities

On the face of it, a warm relationship may seem to be a matter merely of being nice to children. However, it is more than this and it is to the work of Carl Rogers (1961) that we must turn to appreciate what is involved here. There are three personal characteristics considered by Rogers to be desirable qualities in a successful counsellor and it seems that the same qualities are involved in the establishment of a warm relationship; these are described as 'acceptance', 'genuineness' and 'empathy'.

Acceptance

Acceptance means being non-judgemental of the child and accepting his/her personality as it is. But how can a teacher be non-judgemental when a child is misbehaving, one might ask? The answer is that the child is still accepted even though his/her behaviour needs criticism. This is an important difference and is outlined by Gordon (1970; 1974).

It means letting the student know you may disapprove of the behaviour but without devaluing the person. For example, a teacher might say 'I am tired of seeing this mess on the floor,' rather than 'You are still making a mess and I am tired of you doing this'.

The first statement, even if said with anger is not personalized and, therefore, the relationship was not threatened as easily as in the second statement when the student clearly received a message which said there was something wrong with him/her as a person. The teacher should continue to respect the student even if detesting the behaviour.

It might seem a simple enough rule to follow but respect for others cannot easily be faked. Children soon spot those who are not genuine. Unfortunately the quality of acceptance is not one which can be practised. It is more an attitude of mind and a personal philosophy than a technique to be learned. It means genuinely liking people, having a sincere respect for them and a firm belief in the potential ability of people to change.

Genuineness

Genuineness can be developed, although it demands an honest appraisal of one's own personality. It means being able to be spontaneous in social relationships without being defensive. It means being a 'real person' rather than hiding behind a 'professional mask'. To be this way a person has to have high self-esteem and so able to reveal his/her personality without fear of rejection or disapproval. This is not easy when our greatest need is to be liked and when we know that we are not always as competent, skilful or likeable as we would like.

However, it is all too easy to succumb to the temptation of putting on an act. Carl Jung refers to this as 'wearing a persona'. People who do this regularly hide their 'human side' from others and the danger is that, eventually, they hide it from themselves. This is undesirable on two counts: 1) it interferes with communication as people do not meet the real person so do not really trust them; and 2) it is bad for mental health to be cut off from the real person in oneself. This can produce all manner of tensions. Examples of this can be found repeatedly in show business, where actors have to wear a persona in their chosen role. Actors are not noted for stable relationships in their lives.

Once again we are faced with the cultural phenomenon of a high premium being placed on perfection in all things. To be genuine, therefore, will imply the ability to recognize that failure and success are relative terms and that in some sense we are all failures just as in some sense we are all successes.

Empathy

Empathy means being able to appreciate what it feels like to be another person. Whilst none of us could ever wholly know what that would be like we do have sufficient feelings and experiences in common to be able to 'get into another person's shoes' to some degree. Some people are more skilful at this than others, but we can all refine this important skill of communication with practice. Adults should be able more easily to empathize with children having at one time been children themselves!

One useful way of developing empathy is to try to understand the feelings behind a person's words. Usually we are so intent on understanding the verbal message that we can miss knowing just how the person is feeling, and our verbal reply will communicate that we have not really understood the emotional context. The relationship is all the weaker as a result.

Once students feel that the teacher knows what it feels like to be them, they are 'on the teacher's wavelength' and are more likely to trust the teacher and to be influenced by the teacher. Rogers (1975) demonstrates a correlation between the degree of empathy in a student and level of school attainment. Putting this in simple terms, we all tend to do or perform better when we like the teacher and feel that the teacher likes us.

It is worth drawing attention at this juncture to the difference between empathy and identification, as the two can be easily confused. Whereas *empathy* means being able to appreciate what it feels like to be the other person, *identification* means actually behaving like the other person and feeling like the other person. In empathy the teacher remains in the role of teacher and so in charge of the class, even though being able to understand the child's feelings. If there is identification with the student, the teacher becomes 'one of the kids', loses authority and becomes childlike. If the teacher is not sufficiently mature, with high self-esteem, there is always this danger when trying to appreciate the child's world.

Empathy means listening to feelings and may prove to be difficult at times for the busy classteacher. Even simple listening to verbal messages can often be a problem. The distractions of a normal, healthy classroom are frequent and interruptions occur for many reasons. Consider how often an interruption occurs when the teacher is trying to converse with an individual student. A second child may suddenly demand attention for a host of possible reasons ranging from the reasonable to the deliberately disruptive. Visitors enter the room often unannounced. An event may occur outside the room which is momentarily distracting.

To be able to establish an empathic relationship with an individual student the teacher must be on guard against all possible distractions. There is nothing more guaranteed to reduce self-esteem than when the person we are relating to suddenly turns his/her back on us.

Establishing empathy

The work of humanistic psychologists such as Rogers has shown how a child's level of attainment is related to the quality of the relationship he/she has with his/her teacher. This relationship depends on the teacher's ability to empathize with the child. Empathy means knowing what it feels like to be the child, and is often referred to as 'getting on someone's wavelength'. One way of establishing empathy is through listening to feelings and reflecting them. In the following scenes, two children are in distress. In the first scene, the teacher does not empathize with the child, and so the child remains with his distress unresolved. In the second scene, the teacher is aware of the importance of listening and reflecting feelings, and so the child's distress is relieved.

1

Teacher   Why are you crying, Peter?
Peter   It's nothing, Sir (*wiping his eyes*).
Teacher   There must be a reason. Tell me – I may be able to help [responding to the words only].
Peter   It's because I've just lost my pen my Dad bought me.
Teacher   Is that all? I can soon solve that problem. Here – have this one. It's new. I've had it for ages but I don't need it. [Dealing logically with the problem but ignoring feelings.]
Peter   Thank you, Sir (*begins to cry again*).
Teacher   Now what's the matter? [Unable to empathize.]
Peter   Nothing, Sir (*trying not to cry*).
Teacher   Now there must be something else wrong. You don't cry for nothing. What is it? Come now, tell me [continuing to respond logically and to ignore feelings].
Peter   I wish I hadn't lost my other pen (*more crying*).
Teacher   Now you are just being silly. I've given you mine which is just like the one you lost and you still cry [begins to be irritable as not able to empathize].
Peter   I want my pen that my Dad bought me (*sobbing*).
Teacher   Now that's enough. There's no need for that and I've listened to enough crying. Get on with your work [continues to be perplexed].
Peter   (*Trying to hide tears*) Yes, Sir.

2

Teacher   Why are you crying, Peter?
Peter   It's nothing, Sir (*wiping eyes*).
Teacher   You seem unhappy [has listened to feelings].
Peter   I just lost my new pen my Dad bought me.

Teacher I understand. You must be feeling upset about that [communicates has understood].

Peter (*Dries eyes*) It was terrible 'cos my Dad just bought it for my birthday and he hasn't a lot of money.

Teacher I expect you are feeling upset for him as well [continues to empathize].

Peter Yes, he would be sad. A boy knocked it out of my hand and it fell into the lake.

Teacher I know your Dad, I bet he will understand how you feel [gives support through empathy].

Peter Do you really, Sir?

Teacher He seems to be a very kind Dad, so I'm sure he'll be OK about it when you explain things. Accidents do happen [gives further support].

Peter Yes, I suppose so (*brightening up*).

Teacher You're feeling much better about it now, aren't you? [Continues to empathize].

Peter (*Smiling*) Yes, Sir.

Teacher By the way, you can have this one if you like – I've had it for ages, but I've never used it [responds logically to words now that he has empathized].

Peter Thank you, Sir.

The teacher in the first scene was using an immediate and logical approach to the problem. The teacher in the second was using counselling skills to establish a relationship within which Peter would feel understood. The teacher in the first scene completely missed the real problem, which was Peter's feelings for his father. A logical approach like that used by the second teacher was able to establish empathy by listening to the feelings behind the words. The solution was then not one of providing another pen, but rather of helping the boy to understand that he was not alone with his feelings.

Teacher self-esteem

The teacher with high self-esteem is likely to produce students with high self-esteem and also the converse. There is ample evidence to show that people who have positive attitudes towards themselves are also likely to have positive attitudes towards others (Omwake, 1954; Burns, 1975). The personal characteristics in the teacher which contribute to the development of high self-esteem have received some attention in the research (Maslow, 1954).

In addition to the qualities of empathy, acceptance and genuineness already mentioned, it seems that teachers who are able to delegate routine jobs, are able to find time to relate personally to the students, are tolerant of students' conversations and are generally relaxed in their teaching are those who also have high self-esteem. This implies they are able to present a high self-esteem model with which the students identify. It is interesting that this process of identification with the teacher is strongest where the students perceive the teacher as establishing a 'growth-producing atmosphere' (Murray, 1972).

Communication

Non-verbal

As well as the teacher's personal characteristics affecting the student's self-esteem there are other factors within the control of the teacher which also can affect the self-esteem of the student. Amongst these the effect of the teacher's non-verbal behaviour is a particularly powerful influence. Children are very sensitive to non-verbal cues from others and apparently this sensitivity is reduced as the child develops so that the adult in comparison is often totally unaware of non-verbal cues.

Body posture, body orientation, eye contact, pauses in speech, tone and speed of speech, gestures, all can communicate different messages. Research has shown that these non-verbal cues communicate along three dimensions: the extent to which the person likes/dislikes; feels involved/non-involved; feels superior/inferior, to the other (Argyle, 1970).

Whereas verbal statements are generally more objective and

can be manipulated non-verbal behaviour cannot be so easily manipulated as it is more subjective and more instinctive. So even if we try to hide our feelings of dislike they will tend to be communicated non-verbally especially to the person sensitive to non-verbal cues. If a teacher feels a student to be an unpleasant influence in the class but tries to make friends with the student by saying 'I like you', the chances are that the teacher's non-verbal behaviour will be saying the opposite.

The evidence is that when there is this conflict between the verbal and the non-verbal messages it is the non-verbal which is taken notice of. Teachers need, therefore, to check their sincerity – which means, of course, being genuine. This raises another important issue.

What should be done about the student whose behaviour cannot be praised? Does the teacher risk reducing self-esteem by ignoring the student or risk communicating dislike through non-verbal behaviour? The answer to this question has been given already with regard to the desirable qualities which are conducive to self-esteem enhancement, that is, the quality of being able to accept the student even if not the behaviour.

The teacher will need sometimes to reflect deeply on his/her own behaviour before being able to do this. Where it is difficult to accept the student the question must be asked: 'What is it in me that prevents me from giving this student respect even though I do not approve of the behaviour?' This point is discussed further in Chapter 8 in relation to building teacher self-esteem.

Verbal

It is more obvious that verbal messages can either enhance or reduce self-esteem. Staines (1958) identifies the words and phrases teachers use in the classroom and finds that they could be classified into two groups: those that are encouraging, praising, valuing and generally relaxing; and those that are cajoling, blaming, pushing and generally anxiety-producing. The students' self-esteem and also their levels of school attainment were higher in the first group.

It is fairly obvious that the words 'You have done well' are more likely to enhance self-esteem whilst 'You can do better than this' is less likely to do so. Of course, in each case the non-verbal behaviour which accompanies the words is going to influence the final message. It is assumed that the statements in each case are made with sincerity. The conclusion from the Staines's research is that there is a positive and a negative way of saying the same thing and that which is used is crucial in determining its effects on self-esteem.

Teachers often ask whether all this means that the student should never be blamed or chastised. It should be stated categorically that enhancing self-esteem does not mean ignoring poor work or disruptive behaviour. With regard to poor attainments no matter if the teacher does pretend that the child is doing well, the child very quickly compares him/herself with peers and obtains a realistic self-perception. This is why even where some classes are grouped for ability but with an attempt to disguise this by calling the groups anything but A, B, C or the like (for example, fishes, animals) the children soon know which are the 'clever' groups and which are the 'dull' ones.

The main point here, however, is that teachers need to give a student a realistic self-concept, not a false one, and that when the relationship is a caring, trusting one, they will accept blame and criticism without this adversely affecting self-esteem (Sharp and Muller, 1978). Perhaps, more importantly, the teacher should be looking to praise effort and behaviour rather than attainment, although this raises the issue of how far a competitive atmosphere is potentially harmful. Clearly, when the child is being made overanxious by the need to compete then it is harmful for the development of self-esteem.

Maintaining self-esteem

Teacher Come in, John. Sit down, please [communicates respect].

John Thank you, Sir.

Teacher Do you remember why I asked you to come to see me? [Gives opportunity to speak, so communicates trust.]

John Yes, Sir, because I've been in trouble again.

Teacher	That's right. I thought we might have a chat about how best to help you settle down, as your behaviour is causing concern to a lot of people. What do you feel about it? [Separates the boy from the behaviour.]
John	Yes, Sir. I suppose that's true sir.
Teacher	I'm particularly worried in case your behaviour causes you to miss important parts of lessons and you might then have difficulties when it comes to exams. It would be a pity if you failed the exams, as you're an intelligent boy and could do well. Is there anything you'd like to tell me which you think I should know, as I think you look a bit nervous? [Emphasizes the positive; communicates trust.]
John	Yes, Sir. I can't do maths, Sir. I lost my maths book last term.
Teacher	I see. Have you talked to the maths teacher about that? [Communicates trust.]
John	No, Sir. He doesn't know and I daren't tell him.
Teacher	Would you like me to tell him for you? [Gives support.]
John	Would you, Sir?
Teacher	Well of course, if you want me to [places responsibility for action on John].
John	Thank you, Sir.
Teacher	If you have your book, do you think your behaviour would improve? [Emphasizes the positive and potential for change.]
John	Yes, Sir, 'cos then I'd have something to do.
Teacher	OK, John, let's see Mr Jones. I expect he'll be surprised to hear you've not been working because you lost the maths book [communicates understanding].
John	Yes, Sir.
Teacher	Is there anything making you unhappy? We do want all the students here to be happy. Then they work well.
John	No, Sir, I like it here really.

Teacher   OK, John. Thank you for coming to see me. Good-
           bye. [Closes with respect.]
John   Goodbye, Sir.

The teacher displayed

* respect for John throughout the interview
* belief in John's ability to change
* positive attitudes
* good listening skills.

Reducing self-esteem

Teacher   Come in, Smith – sit down (*without looking up*) [no
           eye contact].
John   Thank you, Sir (*sits on edge of chair*).
Teacher   Now let me see. I told you to come and see me
           because you are a badly behaved boy. Do you un-
           derstand? (*Voice rising*) [unable to separate boy
           from behaviour].
John   Yes, Sir (*feeling frightened*).
Teacher   You are the worst boy in the school, right? (*Voice
           harsh and aggressive.*)
John   Yes, Sir.
Teacher   I can't see you passing any exams or getting a good
           job when you leave with your sort of behaviour –
           what do you say? [No confidence in potential for
           change.]
John   No, Sir.
Teacher   So what are we going to do with you, eh? [No
           interest in John as a person.]
John   I don't know, Sir.
Teacher   Well, I'll tell you what. I'm giving you a chance to
           change before it's too late. I'm going to have you sit
           at the front of the class and I want you to come to
           my desk after every lesson. If you have been well
           behaved, I'll give you a star on this card. Under-
           stand? [Communicates lack of trust.]

John	Yes, Sir.
Teacher	Now if you have the sense to behave then you'll earn lots of these stars and when you have 20 of them I'll give you a reward. Do you understand me? [Communicates lack of trust.]
John	Yes, Sir.
Teacher	The reason I'm not expelling you from this school is because I think you just might be able to stop being stupid. If you don't stop, then out you go! See? [Emphasizes the negative.]
John	Yes, Sir.
Teacher	Now do you understand what I'm saying? [Communicates lack of trust.]
John	Yes, Sir.
Teacher	Right! Well, off you go. And for goodness sake try not to look so miserable. Anybody would think you were going to the gallows. Smile, for goodness sake [uses sarcasm].
John	Yes, Sir.
Teacher	Get out! I've looked at you for long enough [confirms the negative] (*John scuttles out*).

The teacher displayed

- lack of trust in potential to change
- lack of respect
- inability to empathize
- superiority of position through body language
- negative attitudes throughout
- use of sarcasm
- *inability to separate John from behaviour*
- *no interest in John as a person*
- *no opportunity for John to contribute, because of poor listening skills.*

Teacher's preferred teaching style

It is not only the teacher's attitude towards the students which affects self-esteem but the teacher's attitudes towards the particular teaching post and organization. In a famous study by Barker-Lunn (1970) it was found that teachers who believed in streaming for ability but had to teach in a mixed-ability situation generally had students with lower attainments and lower self-esteem. Moreover, teachers who believed in mixed-ability teaching and had to teach in a streamed situation also had similar results. It is interesting to reflect in this study that students of above-average ability were not so affected as those of average and below-average ability.

This question of the teacher being 'mismatched' is related to job satisfaction and in turn to stress and self-esteem. This topic is discussed further in Chapter 8.

Expectancy effects

An aspect of the teacher–student relationship which has received a good deal of attention in the literature is that known as 'the expectancy effect'. This refers to the phenomenon that students tend to behave according to the teacher's belief in their worth. According to Hargreaves (1972) teachers generally have an 'ideal pupil' model, and those pupils in their care who do not conform to this ideal model are evaluated unfavourably and are not expected to perform well. The classical study of Rosenthal and Jacobson (1968) shows how this led to pupils fulfilling their teachers' expectations.

The work of Brophy and Good (1974) demonstrates how this occurs. It seems to be natural in all of us to want to classify and categorize people so that we know where we stand with them. Just as nature abhors a vacuum so the psyche will fill in the missing information even if it is on doubtful evidence. Brophy and Good show how teachers seek, from the child's previous teacher, information with regard to work standard and behaviour and then operate on the assumption that the child will conform to this standard. They relate to the child as if they expect this behaviour. The present movement to avoid labelling children in the area of special education is also based on this kind of phenomenon.

Although it has been demonstrated in the research that the teacher may influence the student to behave in ways which the teacher expects, this will only occur where the relationship between them is a close one. Also, when the teacher's expectancies are radically different from the child's perceptions of his/her own behaviour the evidence is that the teacher's expectations are ignored. So the expectancy effect does not occur in all circumstances. However, it is important that teachers are aware of the possibilities of it happening and so will be able to do something about it.

Everyday contacts

Although there are many aspects of the classroom environment which may influence the student's self-esteem, the research shows that it is the teacher's day-to-day contacts with the students which have the greatest effect.

In addition to the kinds of personal relationships already discussed, the teacher should try to ensure that some degree of personal contact is made with all students in the course of the day even if this amounts only to a smile or one word of encouragement. This is easier, perhaps, for the primary teacher who has the children for most of the day rather than for the secondary teacher who may have the students for only an hour a day or less.

It should be the aim of all teachers to get to know each student personally as soon as this is possible. However, this does not mean infringing their rights to privacy. Direct questioning of home life, for instance, should be avoided even when it may be suspected that all is not well at home. In that case the teacher should give the student opportunity to communicate home details through the establishment of a caring, trusting relationship.

From the evidence presented in this chapter, it can be appreciated that all teachers are in a position to enhance self-esteem while teaching and without needing always to think of setting up a systematic programme. Where teachers are genuine, empathic and accepting, they will automatically provide a self-esteem enhancing ethos in the classroom. For those students who have been identified as having low self-esteem and who may have other problems there are activities which can be organized. These are outlined in Chapter 4.

Further reading

Argyle, M. (1994) *Psychology of Interpersonal Behaviour*, Penguin Books, Harmondsworth.

Gordon, T. (1972) *Teacher-effectiveness Training*, Wyden, New York.

Hargie, R., Saunders, J and Dickson, L. (1995) *Social Skills In Interpersonal Communication*, Routledge, London.

Neill, R. (1991) *Classroom Non-verbal Communication*, Routledge, London.

Chapter 4

Classroom activities

Where there is an ethos of acceptance, and where teachers are able to be genuine and empathic, there will be a self-esteem enhancing ethos in their classrooms. However, for some children their self-esteem is so low that this approach will need to be supplemented with a structured programme. It should be emphasized, however, that even where structured programmes are used, those personal qualities in the teacher are still considered to be essential. No programmes or exercises will make the slightest difference to children's self-esteem unless the teacher conducting them possesses the qualities of acceptance, genuineness and empathy. It is of some concern that there are on the open market some published programmes for self-esteem enhancement for use by teachers which appear to ignore this fact. Programmes containing exercises and activities will not by themselves make the slightest difference to a child's self-esteem.

Aims and rationale

The first aim is to allow children to express any feelings which they might normally feel unable to express either through a fear of punishment or through feelings of guilt. The low self-esteem child often lacks spontaneity. There is always the fear that expression of certain feelings, thoughts or ideas will result in disapproval or rejection. Through structured exercises the child gradually learns that it is OK to have feelings and ideas which are different from others and that it does not mean the end of the world if he/she expresses them. Gradually, he/she learns the principle of individuality and learns to have confidence in being different.

The child with certain fears is able to receive the support of the group and may discover for the first time that he/she is not the only person with the same fear. It can be tremendously supportive to realize this.

The second aim is to give experiences of positive feedback. It can be a revelation to the low self-esteem child to hear somebody express positive thoughts about him/her. Low self-esteem children are just not used to hearing these things. With these exercises they gradually begin to perceive themselves in a more positive light.

The third aim is to give opportunity for taking risks. The low self-esteem child cannot take risks either physically or in the sense of revealing his/her own personality. Such children often demonstrate a lack of confidence in all areas of their lives as low self-esteem so easily generalizes at this stage.

Introducing the programme

The way in which a self-esteem enhancement programme is introduced to the children can be crucial in determining the successful outcome of the programme. There have been cases where teachers have simply asked children to form a group and then began to work through the activities, with no preparation at all. There are inevitably going to be anxieties surrounding the operation and these have to be dealt with. Without a proper introduction to the programme the children will be so suspicious of it that it will be almost impossible to establish their trust. Children, just like adults for that matter, can be suspicious of the motives of those who suddenly want them to discuss sensitive issues and to participate in emotionally-toned activities. It is essential therefore that they are properly prepared for the programme. It is suggested that teachers explain to the pupils at the outset that the teacher has noticed that sometimes they do not appear to be very happy in class. As a result, it has been decided to try to help them feel better about themselves and about each other. The precise words used to communicate this message will depend on the age and intellect of the pupils concerned, but the word 'counselling' is probably best left out. In the experiments referred to in

Appendix 1, I simply said to the pupils (aged 8) that I was seeing them 'to ensure that they were happy in school'. A simple explanation is all that is required.

Organizing the sessions

1. Identify those children whose self-esteem has been assessed formally as below average.
2. Choose for the programme no more than eight children.
3. Interview each child individually to explain the programme.
4. Do not insist that the children join the group where there is obvious resistance.
5. If a child resists taking part, try to engage him/her in a counselling programme (see Chapter 5).
6. Set rules for the group, e.g. no put-downs, teacher always has the final say.

Sequence of activities

There are literally hundreds of possible exercises and activities designed to enhance self-esteem. Many of these have been published by various authors and are in use in several schools. Unhappily some teachers have had to report that they do not work (Vipond, 1995). However, on closer examination it has been discovered either, 1) the qualities of acceptance, genuineness and empathy were missing, as discussed earlier; or 2) the programme was administered without regard to the sequence of activities. It is essential that teachers adhere to a strict sequence in the presentation of these activities.

The following sequence of presentation of the exercises should be used:

- Trust activities.
- Expression-of-feelings activities.
- Positive feedback activities.
- Risk-taking exercises.

The programme

Self-esteem is often slow to change and teachers should be prepare for the programme to last a whole term. Each individual session should last no more than 45 minutes. The number of activities conducted under each of the headings listed above will vary according to the needs of the group. Teachers will find that most groups need fewer sessions on the trust activities, perhaps requiring two sessions only, with equal time spent on the other activities spread over the remainder of the term. These are suggestions only, and drawn from the author's previous experiences.

Trust activities

Trusting means being secure enough to be able to express feelings and to be sufficiently secure with one another to be able to count on group support when taking risks. Clearly, the establishment of trust has to be a priority.

It is a good plan to begin the first session with a physical trust activity. Two examples of this type of activity are given below.

Leading the Blind (suitability: primary age)

Children work in pairs. One child is blindfolded while the other leads him/her around the school. Instructions are given that they must not lead their partner into danger. They each take turns at being blindfolded. After the session the group reassembles and a discussion takes place. The following questions should be asked:

- What did it feel like to have to trust their partners while they were blindfolded?
- Why is it that we are not able to trust some people but can easily trust others?
- What qualities do we see in those we can trust?
- What qualities do we see in those we cannot trust?

Catching the Blind (suitability: all ages)

Children to work in pairs. Both are seated with one behind the other. One child is blindfolded and sits waiting for instructions from the second one. The instructions are to lean back with instruction for the second child to catch the first one, so preventing him/her from falling. The group reassembles and again the questions of trust are asked. This time the question should be put to group whether the qualities present in those they trusted not to lead them into danger would be the same qualities they would expect to find in those they feel they can confide in.

Expression of feelings

These activities have two aims: 1) to support children over possible fears and/or anxieties; and 2) to give practice in expressing feelings without guilt.

Sharing Fears, Hopes and Aspirations (suitability: secondary age)

First, working individually, children are asked to complete the following sentences in writing:

- I feel happy when . . .
- I feel sad when . . .
- I feel silly when . . .
- I feel angry when . . .
- I feel afraid when . . .
- I feel glad when . . .
- I feel proud when . .

Next, the children are asked to read out their sentences, dealing with one at a time.

Circle Time (suitability: secondary age)

Children are asked to form a circle with the teacher included. The session is introduced as an opportunity for the children to say anything they like concerning school. They are encouraged to make positive comments as well as negative ones. It may be necessary for the teacher gently to draw out the more reticent members of the group. The teacher makes it clear that their comments will not be criticized or discussed with anybody else outside the session. Most children talk freely once they realize that the proceedings will remain confidential and that the teacher is non-critical. There are only two rules:

1. Nobody must laugh or scoff at anyone else's comments.
2. Permission to speak will be given by the teacher only on a raised hand.

Guess the Emotion (suitability: all ages)

Different emotions are written on pieces of paper prepared by the teacher and placed in a box. Each child in turn draws out a piece and acts out the written emotion, non-verbally. The rest of the group have to guess the emotion.

Recalling the Good Times (suitability: all ages)

Children are asked to recall a time when they felt especially happy. They are asked to close their eyes and visualize the scene. After a few minutes eyes are opened and volunteers are asked to tell the group what it felt like.

Positive feedback

Children with low self-esteem rarely, if ever, hear anybody making positive comments about them. As a consequence they do not at first easily accept positive statements about themselves without some degree of embarrassment. Teachers should be prepared therefore for these exercises to result at first in defensive laughter and strong denial from the objects of any admiration. Despite this, eventually they will make a difference.

Anonymous Praise (suitability: all ages)

Children affix a sheet of paper on each other's backs and then approach one another informally to write on the owner's paper one positive comment about them. This continues until all have had a comment from every member of the group.

Public Praise (suitability: all ages)

Children take it in turns to be the object of admiration from the rest of the group. Seated in a circle each member of the group makes one positive comment about the object of admiration. They are given 30 seconds to say something positive or else they are 'out'. The procedure can be continued a second and even a third time round with most of them having to drop out eventually and the remainders declared the winners.

Positive Postings (suitability: all ages)

Each child has to write on one sheet of paper one statement saying why they like each other. The sheets of paper are then 'posted' to each other for them to take away and read at home.

Taking risks

This is the final stage of activities and provided the group has successfully completed the previous stages improvements in confidence should be in evidence. The taking of risks is probably the most obvious distinction between the low self-esteem and the high self-esteem child. Consequently, these activities will provide the teacher with a measure of how much improvement in self-esteem has been made.

Playing the Expert (suitability: all ages)

Each child is prescribed a role to play in a short dramatic scene. The roles include explorer, map-reader, fire-fighter, arms expert, cook, engineer, and any others which the teacher may wish to include. Any suitable scene could be acted. The following scene has been found to be a popular one. Their task was to rescue an important person captured by outlaws and imprisoned in a remote castle. The castle is guarded by a ferocious animal and is situated on the opposite side of a river infested with crocodiles. The rules of this drama are as follows:

1. The experts have to be consulted before decisions are made in their area of expertise.
2. The expert's advice has to be taken without arguments by the others.
3. Nobody must mock any one.

Playing the Hero/Heroine (suitability: primary age)

Children work in pairs and each takes turns at playing the role of a TV news interviewer. The child is interviewed after having

1. been seen to rescue a drowning person in the sea;
2. just won an Olympic medal;
3. been seen scoring the winning goal in a school's football match; and

4. been the first child to travel to the moon and back.

Addressing the Group (suitability: all ages)

Each child is asked to prepare a short five-minute talk to the group on any topic of his/her choosing. Teacher should give suggestions as to the topic. Most children would probably choose a hobby.

Affirmations

At the end of each session it is useful for the group to close their eyes and say to themselves the following:

- 'I am a happy person.'
- 'I am a confident person.'
- 'I am not afraid.'
- 'People trust me.'
- 'I like me.'
- 'Other people like me.'

In the early stages, the teacher may have to say each sentence first with the children following in unison.

Whole-school approaches

Research into the psychology of groups shows the importance of having a common aim as a significant factor in group morale (Argyle, 1970). When group morale is high, individuals' self-esteem also tends to be high. Any activities, therefore, which result in a building of morale in the school are likely to enhance self-esteem. The feeling of belonging to a worthwhile group should be the aim of the whole-school approach to self-esteem enhancement. The ways in which this can be achieved obviously will depend on many factors, including the type and size of the school as well as the neighbourhood. The following are among the means by which some schools have raised morale in this way.

Self-esteem through physical performance

As most teachers know full well, the child who achieves in physical pursuits usually has high self-esteem. It is interesting to reflect on the high premium our society continues to place on physical prowess. How many children, or adults for that matter, would rather regularly represent their country in an international sport than achieve in some intellectual pursuit? Unfortunately, most of us lack the talent to be able to do this. However, we can go some way towards the same result through fun-runs, bike trials, school camps.

Whatever activity is chosen the aim should be for the whole school to take part. Clearly this has to be organized so that the weaker members of the school do not suffer unduly. The fun-run could be organized so that each year-group completed a different part of the course, each part being of different lengths. Everybody who has taken part should be presented with a certificate to that effect. If, in addition, a sponsor can be found money could be earned or donated to a charity.

Self-esteem through the school concert

The school concert or musical event is often a regular feature in a school's calendar but rarely does the whole school take part. This kind of event could be organized so that even those who do not actually perform on stage can still take a part in the production. If the event is made open to the public then it becomes easier to involve everybody, for example, classes taking turns at different performances to function as ushers. Once again, the essential aim is for the whole school to be involved and for there to be a tangible recognition of this. Each child could, for instance, be sent a letter of thanks afterwards.

Curriculum activities

Whereas all teaching can be organized within a self-esteem enhancement framework some subjects can be intrinsically self-enhancing. Examples of these are music, art, drama, creative writing. If, in addition, children are given an opportunity to discuss their feelings when engaged in these activities then further self-enhancement is possible.

Developing internal locus of control

The term 'locus of control' was first introduced by Rotter (1954). It refers to a dimension of personality which ranges from one extreme of a belief by an individual that whatever happens to him/her is not within his/her control. At the other extreme of the continuum the individual believes that whatever happens to him/her is completely within his/her control. The former is known as being 'externally controlled' and the latter is known as being 'internally controlled'.

For an example of the internally controlled pupil consider this likely comment on passing an examination: 'I expected to pass as I worked very hard and so I am not surprised at the results.' Failing the examination his/her comment might have been: 'I failed this examination because I am pretty stupid even though I worked hard.' It can be appreciated that the extreme position is perhaps unrealistic. The externally controlled pupil might have said on passing the examination: 'I was very lucky, and anyway I think they were being kind to me.' The same pupil might have said on failing the examination: 'I failed because I had a rotten teacher.' Clearly, some degree of internality is preferable to externality.

For the purpose of self-esteem enhancement it is useful to know that there is a positive correlation between internality, self-esteem and achievement. We should aim therefore to help pupils achieve some feeling of control over their destinies. In the class-room this can be developed in three main ways:

1. Through pupils having some say in their own governance, that is, the setting up of class rules.
2. Through the giving of opportunities for the recording and the evaluating of their own progress.
3. By giving some opportunities to initiate their own learning.

In a joint study (Lawrence and Blagg, 1974) a group of children who were allowed to control part of their remedial reading sessions through reading games showed greater gains in both reading and self-esteem than other matched groups. Although locus of control was not measured in that particular study a number of studies have shown how teachers can teach pupils to become more 'internal' and in turn increase their attainments (de Charms, 1976).

In class discussions teachers should encourage pupils to be critical of their own learning environment and the ways in which their learning is organized. The aim should be to help them become responsible for their own behaviour, with regard of course to their stage of development. It would be unrealistic, for instance, to expect the first-year primary child to be able to discuss the organization of the classroom without having had the experience of working in groups.

Active tutorial work

In Chapter 1 we referred to the symbolic interactionist view of the 'self' concept. People in general are group dependent and self-concept is formed partly by social interaction. As the classroom comprises a particular group the teacher is in an ideal position to be able to structure the group to the best advantage of the pupils.

The primary aim of the classroom group normally is academic achievement but as all teachers know, social learning takes place at the same time as the pupils interact with one another. In active tutorial work the learning of social interaction is the main focus. This kind of group activity is similar to Circle Time but differs in two important respects. First, it is more structured in that the teacher has a clear teaching objective, for example, to help pupils appreciate the dangers of smoking. Secondly, the teacher takes a more prominent role and acts as a model.

For this activity to be successful, the teacher needs to have a healthy self-concept and so be able to participate in self-disclosure and to deal effectively with hostile views when expressed without becoming defensive (see Chapter 8). When setting up the group there are the following four basic considerations.

The size of the group

For most of the self-esteem enhancement activities a group of around eight seems to work best. Most teachers have had experience of group work and no doubt will organize the numbers according to their own experience with a particular class.

Personality differences

The first consideration should be to ensure that the more reticent members of the class are not grouped with the more dominant ones. There is evidence to support the view that like person-alities work best together, for example, extroverts and introverts should be separated for this kind of activity. It is a mistake to assume that a shy individual will be 'brought out of his/her shell' by sitting next to a more outgoing pupil.

Friendship

Within the broad extrovert/introvert groups there will be par-ticular friendships. These should be identified and put together.

Abilities

Clearly it would be unwise to place a slow-learning pupil alongside a high-flyer. Discussion is always smoother when the group comprises roughly pupils of the same intelligence level. This is not meant to imply that in other types of group with different aims mixed abilities should not work together. Indeed, there is a good case for arguing that pupils with particular hand-icaps should be integrated with non-handicapped pupils when possible. For the purpose of this activity, however, it is best to group like with like.

Conducting the group

Following a brief introduction by the teacher on the aims of the session the group is asked to comment. Various views will be expressed, some of them in a disparaging way. The teacher must be alert for that kind of comment which can be self-esteem re-ducing for some members of the group. The teacher should deal with a 'put down' by modelling the appropriate behaviour. In this way the teacher takes a more dominant role than in Circle Time. Negative views should be discussed objectively. Sooner or later the teacher will be asked for his/her views, and the teacher should be open and spontaneous and able to express opinions easily without prejudice or defensive behaviour.

Sometimes silences will occur. They can be used positively as when thinking of a particular point which has just been raised. When they become uncomfortable they should be discussed openly. It is of note that in general children are more easily able to tolerate silences than are adults.

When conflicts occur or when members become hostile, it is important for the teacher to intervene to keep the discussion on the topic but without discouraging the expression of feelings. A conflict is an ideal opportunity for the teacher to model the desired behaviour. Pupils can learn much from the mature, high self-esteem teacher who handles this kind of situation effectively, for example, by demonstrating that it is OK to have opposing views, indeed people are perfectly entitled to do so, but there is no need for them to become personal.

This kind of activity is best used with secondary age pupils although it may be successful with brighter primary pupils. The key to its success is the maturity of the teacher. It may seem to some teachers to be a threatening experience but it is well worth the risks. When successful it becomes a growth-producing experience both for the pupils and the teacher.

Reminder

Whatever activities or exercises are used these should be organized and implemented within the framework of acceptance and respect for the student which was discussed in Chapter 3. It is a case of 'not what you do, but the way that you do it'. That quotation is even more apt when considering setting up a counselling programme as described in Chapter 5.

Further reading

Barbra, M. and Barbra, A. (1978) *Self-esteem: a classroom affair.* Winston Press, Minneapolis.

Canfield, J. and Wells, H. (1976) *One Hundred Ways To Enhance Self-concept in the Classroom.* Prentice-Hall, Englewood Cliffs, New Jersey.

Everhart, R.B. (1985) On feeling good about oneself: practical ideology in schools of choice. *Sociological Education,* Vol. 58, pp. 251–260.

Flowers, J.V. (1991) A behavioural method of increasing self-confidence in elementary school children: treatment and modelling results. *British Journal of Educational Psychology,* Vol. 61, pp. 13–18.

Chapter 5

A counselling approach

In Chapter 1 we saw how a counselling approach is successful in enhancing self-esteem and also reading attainment. This kind of programme could be set up in most schools for the type of child or student who is likely to benefit. First, it is important to define what is meant by counselling in this context as counselling can take place at many different levels. It can range from what is sometimes referred to as the 'Dutch Uncle' variety, usually given by a friend or relative who is known to be a good listener, to the highly skilled professional.

In the experiment mentioned, counselling was aimed specifically at changing the children's self-attitudes and not aimed at helping them to resolve any possible emotional or behavioural difficulties. As such it did not demand the insights or training of the professional and so was carried out in the event by non-professionals. That is not to imply that this kind of counselling should be conducted only by non-professionals. The experiments are meant to highlight the personal characteristics considered by the humanist school (Rogers, 1969) to be the essential ingredients in communication.

Teachers who possess these ingredients to a greater or lesser degree should in theory be even more skilled than the non-professional when counselling students with low self-esteem. At whatever level of counselling there is some evidence to indicate that the personal qualities of the counsellor are the keys to effective counselling and not the length of professional training (Carkhuff and Truax, 1967).

The kind of counselling recommended in this chapter is in many ways a replication of an ideal parent–child relationship, and it is theoretically an attempt to combine the theories of Rogers (1951) and Bandura (1977). It acknowledges the need for particular personal skills of communication and also the phenomenon of modelling. The student will model on the counsellor and this will be most effective when the counsellor is also able to establish a warm, caring, empathic relationship.

Introducing the programme to the student

The manner in which the programme is to be introduced to the student is important and care should be taken to do this before the first session. Whatever is said to the student should be said in a non-threatening, low-key manner. The details of the introduction will depend on the age and maturity of the child but in general the following words are suggested: 'I am trying to see as many children as I can to ensure that they are happy in school and as it is not easy to talk in front of others in the class I am seeing children by themselves where possible. Would you like to come along every week?' This is a fairly innocuous introduction, but it does convey that the teacher is interested in the child's welfare and is not intending to test or to teach.

The teacher should also remember the non-verbal cues which the child will be aware of, so the introduction should be accompanied with a smile, and the like. It is also useful, and perhaps wise, to mention the programme to the parents in the same low-key manner. When the teacher is sincere and feels an interest in the counselling approach, the child's response is usually positive.

It should be stated, however, that there are aspects of the teacher's previous relationship with the child which may interfere with the new counselling relationship, which is unique. The child is likely to have perceived the teacher as an authority figure and it may take a few sessions before being able to accept the different non-judgemental relationship. The teacher should be prepared, therefore, for this response and not become anxious about it. Sometimes this may be a serious impediment to the counselling and in that case it is advisable to enlist a teacher from another class to do the counselling or even to introduce a non-professional, as in the experiments referred to earlier.

Whether the teacher or a non-professional is used there are certain principles which should be observed.

Obtaining trust

For many children the counselling relationship is probably a strange experience as they have the luxury of one adult to value and listen to them. As a result they may be a little suspicious at first and be uncommunicative. It is essential that the teacher or non-professional counsellor is prepared for this kind of reaction and does not immediately begin forcing the child to talk. It should be communicated to the child that the teacher knows that it is sometimes difficult to know what to say. Instead of pursuing the topic a game might be introduced or a drink and a biscuit suggested. Anything that will reduce tension should be used. The essential point is to divert the interview into a more relaxed channel. Eventually the child will realize the unique nature of the interview and that it is not threatening. The teacher should, of course, explain that it is confidential.

Future sessions

Once the first session has been completed it will be helpful if the counsellor checklist is used. The insights gained from the checklist should make it easier to structure the remaining sessions. The framework will depend on the personality and interests of the children as well as their maturity level. Some will chat freely, whereas others will need the stimulus of another medium such as a book or a game. Whatever medium is used, it is the *quality* of the relationship which will determine its successful outcome and not the *content*.

The aim is to seek every opportunity to value the child and this is best done through the teacher showing pleasure in the child's company. Where the child may present negative or even unpleasant comments it should be remembered that beneath the unpleasant exterior there is probably a low self-esteem inadequate child. This means the teacher will be able to tolerate and accept the child even though not approving of the behaviour.

The conversation should then take the form of discussing the negative comments within an atmosphere of trust and acceptance. When possible the teacher should attempt to give the child insight into his/her behaviour but without adopting a judgemental attitude. Suggestions should be offered, for instance, rather than advice given.

Counsellor checklist

Towards ensuring effective communications

Non-verbal behaviour
- Do you tend to adopt a 'closed manner' when addressing the student, for example, arms folded?
- Do you use eye contact?
- Do you smile a lot?
- Is your voice harsh and aggressive?

Listening skills
- Do you allow yourself to be distracted?
- Are you able to guess the student's feelings when he/she talks to you?
- Do you 'feed back' to the student the feelings you guess?
- Are you able to paraphrase the student's words as an aid to empathy?

Establishing trust
- Are you able to show the student that you trust him/her?
- Are you able to express your own feelings freely?
- Do the students know the kind of person you are?
- Do you communicate that you are interested in the student as a person?

Being positive
- Are you able to manage difficult behaviour without reducing self-esteem?
- Are you able to change your negative thoughts to positive ones?
- Do you find yourself using more negative than positive phrases?
- Do you have a wide variety of positive phrases and words or only a few?

Developing expectancies
- Do you communicate that you have confidence in the student's ability to learn?
- Do you communicate that you expect the student to behave appropriately?
- Are you able to communicate expectancies without 'commands' and without 'preaching'?
- Are you able to encourage independent thinking in the student?

Respect for privacy

One aim of the programme should be to help the child express feelings. It is a mistake however to force the child to express them. It can be damaging to self-esteem to force people to 'get it off your chest'. This is a commonly heard exhortation, but unless the individual is ready and trusts the person he/she is communicating with, it can be inferior inducing. We all need a private world and if another enters it without invitation we feel threatened.

In the counselling programme the aim should be to provide a trusting relationship within which the child can feel free to confide his/her innermost feelings *should he/she wish to do so*. Statements such as 'Tell me about your parents!' should be avoided even if the teacher has reason to believe that things are not right at home. Instead, the teacher might say 'Sometimes children find it hard to settle in school because they are thinking about their family'. This gives the child the opportunity to say something about his/her family if he/she wants to do so. It also allows the child to change the topic if he/she wishes.

Personality clashes

One reason for misunderstandings between people lies in their different temperaments. We have all had the experience of not being able to relate easily to somebody without really knowing why this is so. We may say 'I can't get on his wavelength', and this is sometimes referred to as a 'personality clash'. The teacher should be prepared for this to occur from time to time.

Common among the differences in personality is that between the introvert and the extrovert. Consider how often we have heard an introvert saying about an extrovert 'Don't trust *that* one. Hail-fellow-well-met. No depth'. The extrovert will also be likely to say 'Don't trust *that* one. Still waters run deep'. Each mistrusts the other because each cannot understand the other's perspective on life. When this clash occurs between teacher and child it is wise to accept it and perhaps use another person to do the counselling.

Avoid patronizing

There is always the danger of sounding patronizing when caring about somebody in distress. The teacher should beware showing the child *sympathy* when what is needed is *understanding*. Sympathy can so easily degenerate into a sentimental sharing of emotions with nothing being done to enhance self-esteem. The aim of the counselling is to influence the child's attitudes towards a positive self-appraisal. Admittedly, the child will bask in the warm emotions which sympathy portrays but this is merely indulgence and in no way contributes to a more positive self-appraisal.

When a child does show negative feelings towards self, for example, 'I'm no good', the teacher should obviously support the child over the circumstances but should not do so in a maudlin or pitying way. That kind of comment should be met preferably with a discussion on the reasons for the statement. If it is seen subsequently as a manifestation of a general feeling of unworthiness and with no rational basis, further discussion should cease on the topic.

Showing interest and listening

The low self-esteem students are unused to having the luxury of finding an important adult who is prepared to listen to them and who also finds them interesting. It is all too easy to miss the significance of the student's need to feel that he/she has a worthwhile opinion. Be on the alert therefore for the smallest signs of an opinion from the student and comment on it by actually saying 'That is an interesting thing to say'.

Beware also the many distractions which can occur when trying to concentrate on the student's comments. There is nothing more inferior inducing than being told to 'Wait a minute while I deal with this'. The student should expect to have the teacher's full attention during the counselling.

We have all had the experience, surely, of colleagues or companions being distracted when we are trying to obtain their attention. Sometimes they are distracted by their own thoughts as when remembering an appointment and then looking at their watch instead of looking at us! Whilst for most people this would be just dismissed as an irritation, for people of low self-esteem it serves to confirm to them that they are inferior.

Length of sessions

Most students require around five minutes to adjust to the session. After a further 30 minutes or so they tend to become restless. It is suggested from experience that each session lasts 40 minutes. It is important to inform the students of this at the outset of the programme and to adhere to it. One main reason for a set time is to avoid the situation where the teacher will have to decide arbitrarily that time is up and so leave the student sometimes wondering if it was something that occurred during the interview which had decided the teacher to end it just at that point. Accordingly it is wise to warn the student that there are 10 minutes left so he/she is not unprepared.

Terminating the programme

It is difficult to be precise regarding the number of sessions the student will need. Ideally, they should continue as long as the student obviously needs them. This is usually shorter than the length of the time the student is continuing to enjoy them. Whilst a permanent programme would probably be enjoyable for most students (it is interesting to observe how they look forward to the sessions), it is not always possible to organize this. The teacher must seek the opinions of colleagues as well as being guided by his/her own observations as to the time to cease.

Once a decision has been made to discontinue the programme it is essential that the student is informed of this decision in such a way that it is not perceived by the student as rejection. Reference should be made to the student's apparent improvement obviating the need for further counselling. Moreover it is always best to begin to discontinue the programme gradually, for example, weekly sessions becoming fortnightly sessions, and then going to once a month until eventually they cease altogether.

At the final session the student should be informed that he/ she and the teacher will always remain friends and that the student should remember to come to see the teacher at a personal level when needed. The teacher need not fear that this is going to result in further impromptu sessions; experience has shown that this happens only when the student genuinely does have a further problem.

If the decision to terminate the sessions has been made wisely then the student will no longer need to come and further contact can remain at the same level of personal involvement as with the rest of the class during everyday teaching.

Using non-professionals

Where the classteacher may find it impossible to do the counselling him/herself, it is worth exploring the use of non-professionals as illustrated in the experiments in Appendix 1.

Obviously it would be important to select these people carefully. Although it is possible to select through the various personality questionnaires available (Rogers, 1961), it is suggested that, apart from the unreliability factors inherent in most methods, to have a formal selection procedure has dangers and could prove to be counterproductive. It would be potentially harmful to have to reject those who did not measure up as suitable.

The selection of non-professional counsellors would, therefore, be made simply on the basis that they are already known to the school as sympathetic to the needs of children without being sentimental, are without any signs of emotional ill-health and, where possible, are emotionally spontaneous. To be able to select people on these criteria requires an intimate knowledge of them. In the experiments referred to earlier the selection was left to the heads of the schools. These were sometimes parents of the children in the school but always people known and recommended by the school principal.

When it has been decided to use non-professionals it is essential that they are prepared to consider the principles outlined in this book and are briefed on at least four separate occasions before the programme begins. It would be useful if the local school psychologist were available to do this and also to meet the counsellors from time to time to monitor the programme. Whilst this is not essential when the teacher has time to do it, in practice it is always best if the teacher is able to call on the services of another professional for support. Whatever is decided upon in this context it is absolutely imperative that the counsellors receive some introduction to self-concept theory and instructions on the logistics of setting up the programme as outlined earlier.

The counselling setting

The remarks under this subheading apply equally to teachers and to non-professionals. The work of researchers, such as Argyle (1970), shows that in addition to needing to be able to establish a warm, caring relationship, those who more easily are able to change attitudes also have *status*. This means that the student should feel that the counsellor is important. In turn the student will feel important by virtue of having an 'important friend'. Translated into practice this implies that the counselling should take place in a comfortable, well furnished room and that the counsellor should be introduced properly by the head of the school.

The issue of status raises once again the point mentioned in Chapter 3 in connection with the teacher's self-esteem, that is, the importance of genuineness. The counsellor should be able to be genuine and spontaneous. In this way he/she will bring into the conversations her/his own lifestyle and interests. This again serves the purpose of making the student feel important.

Selecting the students

The kind of students who respond best to counselling are generally those with at least average intelligence and so are able more easily to reflect on their behaviour and take action on the reflection. It is theoretically possible to select by standardized methods, although perhaps the best way to get to know if a student has low self-esteem is to get to know that student personally. The whole question of assessing self-esteem is addressed in Chapter 2.

The counsellor checklist should be used after the first session with the student.

Further reading

Cowie, H. and Pecherek, A. (1994) *Counselling: Approaches & Issues in Education*. Fulton, London.
Harris, T. (1969) *I'm OK – You're OK*. Pan Books, London.
Priestley, P. and McGuire, J. (1983) *Learning To Help*. Tavistock Publications, London.
Rogers, C. (1951) *Client-centred Therapy*. Houghton Mifflin, Boston.

Chapter 6

Behavioural difficulties

Surveys into the sources of stress in teaching regularly quote having to cope with behavioural difficulties as a major concern. Whilst those teachers who have high self-esteem are more likely to be able to cope than teachers with low self-esteem, students with severe behavioural problems often require intensive treatment. In the not too distant past, treatment usually meant referral to a child guidance clinic and the student would be treated outside the school. More recently some doubt has been cast on the effectiveness of that traditional approach and evidence has accumulated to indicate that more often than not the best person to do the 'treatment' is the classteacher and the best setting for the treatment is in the situation where the problems occur, that is, the classroom.

Whilst the details of treatment and strategies for helping students with behavioural difficulties lie outside the scope of this book the framework within which these helping strategies should be applied is certainly associated with the topic of self-esteem. In all the teacher's relationships with students the teacher communicates acceptance or rejection even though he/she may not always be aware of this. When a student is a behaviour problem and may be impinging on the teacher in an unpleasant way there is always the danger of dealing with the behaviour in such a way that reduces self-esteem, and then the problem can so easily escalate.

Before considering this further it is important to emphasize that enhancing self-esteem is not inconsistent with good discipline. A concern of some teachers has been that by focusing on the quality of their relationship with the students they are in some danger of losing their authority. This is a fallacy although an understandable concern. It is only where the teacher *identifies* rather than *empathizes* with the student that problems with discipline can occur. Teachers must remain in charge of their classroom and if they identify with a student they then become like the student and if the student has a problem both finish up with a problem! The teacher has to learn to communicate to the student that his/her problems are understood and that the teacher knows what it feels like to be that student (empathy), but not to the extent that the teacher loses his/her identity as the person in charge.

There are many methods of achieving class control and most teachers are fully aware of them. Whatever methods are used the aim should be that ultimately the student should take responsibility for his/her own behaviour. This will occur sooner or later depending on the age and maturity of the student provided that the teacher is able to maintain control without reducing self-esteem.

The disruptive student

When a student is disruptive in class the manner and words used by the teacher will determine the effects on the student's self-esteem. When it is possible to control the student's behaviour without reducing self-esteem the future relationship between teacher and student will not be placed at risk. The model suggested here is similar to that recommended by Gordon (1974).

Reducing self-esteem

A child has accidentally upset the contents of your bookcase. Books and equipment are strewn all over the floor and you are naturally upset. The child hurriedly picks them up and replaces them in any order.

Task: A takes the role of child, and B the role of adult. Then A and B reverse roles.

Adult You are stupid. Why didn't you look where you were going? [Uses 'you' message.]

Child Sorry.

Adult You really are an idiot! You never think before doing anything.

Child Sorry.

Adult You really are clumsy, but never mind. You'll grow up one day, I expect.

Child (*Mumbling quietly*) Huh! I hate this place. [Child responds negatively feeling under attack.]

Maintaining self-esteem

Adult I feel so angry when that kind of thing happens as I can never find books easily when they are out of order like that.

Child Sorry.

Adult When I need a book quickly and I find it's not where I expect to find it, I get really cross [uses I–when–because].

Child Sorry, I'll put them back properly for you. [Child responds positively as not under attack.]

Adult Oh! I'll help you. It'll be quicker if we both do it together.

Child I really am sorry. I didn't do it on purpose.

Adult I know. Don't worry – it's just that I get annoyed when I can't find anything.

Child I'll try not to put them out of order.

Adult Thanks. We'll soon put them back.

Child (*Mumbling quietly*) I must try not to do it again.

In the first scene, self-esteem was reduced. In the second scene, self-esteem is maintained, because the adult uses the format 'when–I–and–the reason'. The adult is using 'you' messages in the first scene, and 'I' messages in the second (Gordon, 1974).

First of all a distinction has to be made between the student who is disruptive and enjoying it and the student who is disruptive and tense and perhaps depressed about it.

Mischievousness

Students often 'test out the teacher' to see how far they can go before the teacher sets the limits. This is seen more often in the primary-school child but also in the immature secondary-age student. Children have no natural sense of knowing how to behave appropriately and when parents sometimes have not properly fulfilled this teaching function it is left to teachers to do it. This kind of child is gleefully mischievous and can cause considerable disruption. As a result the teacher is likely to feel considerable anger in return.

It is suggested here that in the interests of establishing a genuine relationship as well as in the interests of the teacher's self-esteem, this anger should be expressed and not hidden. It is the way in which it is expressed that is important. It needs to be expressed in such a way that conveys that it is the behaviour of the student that is the object of the teacher's anger and not the student. This is a subtle but important difference. The following words illustrate: 'I am angry when I see paper thrown around the room.' The key words are *I* and *when*. Usually at this point the student will respond with appropriate behaviour. If instead of these words the following were used, 'You are being silly', then the student immediately recognizes the personal attack and self-esteem is threatened. The whole situation then is in danger of escalation.

Using this approach for this kind of student will usually be sufficient to establish order but this is not meant to imply that the student's behaviour will for ever after be as desired. Some students may need several shows of anger before conforming and may need a more systematic treatment approach involving 'contracts'. In the example discussed here it is the 'surface behaviour' which is the topic of control. But it will at least allow the lesson to continue.

Tension and/or depression

Turning now to the second kind of disruptive behaviour – the student who is not enjoying it and is perhaps tense and perhaps depressed – the immediate aim is to 'take the heat out' of the situation. The point is that this student is probably already in a highly emotional state and if not already of low self-esteem is certainly vulnerable.

Bearing in mind again the need not to reduce self-esteem the teacher needs to reassure the student that he/she knows how the student is feeling. This means empathizing with the student and the teacher may say 'I understand that you are unhappy' or 'I can see that you are feeling miserable about this'. Immediately the student recognizes an attempt to see things from his/her point of view and will calm down a degree. The situation is not left at that as the teacher should then offer to discuss with the student the reasons for the problem, but at the end of the lesson. Again, this allows the lesson to continue and is dealing at this juncture with the 'surface behaviour only'.

It would, of course, be simpler for the teacher to establish control through the threat of punishment, but this only serves to reduce self-esteem. Whilst there is a place in control for punishment particularly in the sense of experiencing the teacher's anger as described, having to rely on punishment as the only method of control means usually that the teacher is unable to establish the caring atmosphere recommended. This means that the students are likely to develop low self-esteem.

Class control which centres on self-esteem enhancement will use positive methods with the teacher providing a calm, high self-esteem model. There will be a healthy learning environment within which the students will feel free to ask questions and to take risks as they learn new skills. They will not be afraid of failing as they use trial-and-error learning and will gain in confidence as they are allowed to work at their own pace and receive the teacher's approval for effort.

In contrast, a teacher who relies on punishments to control the class may indeed have a quiet, well behaved class but the students' natural curiosity will remain inhibited. When they are confronted outside with disruptive behaviour in others they will be likely to respond in terms of the model they have learned in the classroom. They have been taught aggression.

Consistent with this self-esteem enhancement approach to behavioural difficulties is the belief that students are potentially capable of controlling their own behaviour. This is in contrast to the view that implies that students with disturbing behaviour cannot help themselves. If they really are that disturbed they should not be in a school and are in need of psychiatric care. It should be stated here that students who come under that category are rarer than used to be thought and form approximately only 1 per cent of all cases referred to educational psychologists.

It can usually be assumed therefore that the student can be held responsible for his/her behaviour even if it may need the teacher to organize a regular counselling programme to enable the student to gain insight. When that is indicated it should always be done in conjunction with the school psychologist although the principles discussed in connection with counselling of students with learning difficulties and low self-esteem equally apply.

Indeed, once a student is able to establish a caring relationship with a teacher very often the student's problems clear up. Research points to the significance of this kind of relationship in a school when students' home backgrounds may be disturbed (Rutter *et al.*, 1979). The incidence of behavioural difficulties has a stronger association with the quality of the teacher–student relationships in a school than with the students' socioeconomic backgrounds. It is no longer justifiable to comment 'What can you expect – look at the child's home background' when confronted with a behavioural difficulty. The evidence is very clearly in favour of the view that 'schools do make a difference'.

Defence mechanisms against low self-esteem

Obviously 'prevention' is better than 'cure' and the occurrence of many behaviour difficulties could be minimized through the establishment of the kind of positive and caring learning environment which is the main theme of this book. There are some children, however, who will present behaviour difficulties no matter how much effort is put in by the teacher to prevent them. Since the days of Sigmund Freud it has been recognized that sometimes we behave in an irrational manner as a result of unconscious conflicts. Some children may receive threats to their self-esteem emanating from outside the classroom but which are unconsciously expressed as behaviour difficulties within the classroom.

Most of us at some time or other have been victims of the 'kick the cat' syndrome. We may have had a bad day and arrive home tired and frustrated. We feel bad-tempered; unfortunately our aggression is taken out on the nearest object and the cat gets it! Of course, we feel guilty immediately afterwards knowing we have behaved irrationally. Children can be subject to the same phenomenon. There are many different kinds of defence reactions, all attempting in some way to compensate for threats to self-esteem. The following are some of them.

Belittling and blaming others

Most teachers have had to put up with the pupil who continually blames others for his/her difficulties. Jane was in her third year of secondary school and although performing at an average level in most subjects she was not a popular girl. Her behaviour to the teacher was usually polite but she was always complaining to the teacher that other girls were preventing her from working, or that they were not working properly themselves.

Not surprisingly, people quickly lost patience with her and the teacher began to apply sanctions whenever she was out of her seat to complain. This made matters worse and the climax came when she threw her books across the room in a fury having been told by the teacher that she would have to remain behind after school to complete unfinished work. Wisely, the teacher avoided a confrontation seeing that the girl was out of control; the teacher picked it up with the comment 'We can talk about this after school', and quickly changed the topic addressing the whole class. This had the desired effect of calming the girl, and not losing face in front of the class.

This example serves to illustrate how some pupils' behaviour quickly escalates from being at first only mildly irritating. Mildly irritating behaviour like this should be investigated early when it is seen to be persisting, as it can often be, as in this case, a sign of some deeper unconscious conflict.

The example also serves to illustrate that low self-esteem is often manifested by a need to blame others for one's own feelings of inadequacy.

Treatment

Following this scene Jane was interviewed after school by the teacher. In this case the teacher has attended a course on counselling and was well aware of the need to establish a trusting relationship and to maintain Jane's self-esteem. At first she was resistant to discussing anything but gradually relaxed as she became aware that this was not a punitive interview. She agreed to talk further with the teacher the next day and a series of sessions were arranged.

It transpired that at home Jane had always felt inferior to her sister who was younger but seemed to be brighter. Basically she had a good relationship with her sister so never felt able to express negative feelings. Also, her parents made her feel guilty if ever she showed signs of aggression towards her sister. Aggression was therefore repressed but came out in school when with other girls who probably unconsciously reminded Jane of her relationship with her sister.

With Jane's consent her parents were seen by the teacher and they were helped to see how she was developing low self-esteem. They agreed to discuss the problem with a social worker who aimed to help them modify their attitudes towards Jane.

The teacher continued to counsel Jane to help her take responsibility for her own behaviour as well as helping her regain lost self-respect. She began to interfere with other girls' work a lot less frequently and as a result began to gain their respect. As the weeks passed Jane improved out of all recognition as she was able to see that she has been her own worst enemy in the past, and as the parents began to give her more value.

Lying and boastful behaviour

John was in his last year at primary school. He was performing at a slightly below average level in schoolwork but was quite popular with the class. His only real problem was that he regularly told the most outrageous lies and tended to boast about his exploits. The other pupils just laughed at John's stories but new teachers were always taken in at first, for example, 'I went hang-gliding at the weekend with my Dad. We went on the same glider and swooped over the city houses'.

During class discussion periods John always tried to dominate with further tall stories. Sooner or later the class would become scornful and the teacher sarcastic. He would then burst into tears still protesting he was telling the truth. The situation became worse as time went on, until he began to live most of the time it seemed in a fantasy world.

The parents were seen by the teacher and confessed to having the same problems with him at home. It was a happy family and there was no obvious reason for the boy's difficult behaviour. But it was clear that John was for ever trying to say, in effect, 'Take notice of me! I am important!'

John's case serves as an example of how low self-esteem can be masked by an apparent confidence. Despite the boy's accounts of his exploits it was obvious to all that beneath his brash exterior he felt very inadequate.

Treatment

It is not always possible to establish the causes of a behaviour difficulty as in John's case. But it is not always necessary to have to do so if we consider the case from a self-concept theory viewpoint. Here we have a boy who needed a quick boost to his self-esteem and also who had to be helped to appreciate the impact on others of his lying.

As with Jane's case, the treatment centred on, first, the establishment of a trusting relationship between John and his teacher within which he felt able to confide. As he came to trust the teacher he was able to accept the teacher's view that his behaviour had been undesirable and to be able to take responsibility in changing it.

Changes did not occur immediately and whenever he lied thereafter teacher and parent would treat it lightly and quickly change the subject, as distinct from their previous reactions which had been punitive. He was learning a more 'realistic self-image'.

Daydreaming

Peter was 9 years of age and working well below average in schoolwork. He had been referred for a psychological examination with the possibility of a transfer to a special school for slow-learning children. Testing, however, revealed an ability far above that which he had been showing.

Discussion with the classteacher revealed that he daydreamed a lot and was exasperating in that he invariably produced a blank sheet of paper at the end of the lesson when all the other children had done at least four or five sides of work. Peter had been chastised regularly and became used to being punished for 'lack of effort and laziness'.

This is a classical example of the low self-esteem child lacking in confidence and so performing as though of low ability. Peter had opted for avoidance of what he felt to be a potentially humiliating experience. To describe any child as lazy is an evasion of a diagnosis and this was no exception. He scored at a very low level on the 'Lawseq' self-esteem questionnaire and clearly had very little confidence in himself.

It is better to risk the teacher's punishments than to be humiliated in public by being seen to fail. This kind of case often 'represses' the feelings of inadequacy, or in everyday language 'he has shut off'.

Treatment

The school psychologist organized counselling and self-esteem enhancement activities as a starter. Soon Peter began taking more notice of his surroundings and to begin to attempt to work. At that point remedial reading was arranged as he was now in a more positive frame of mind to benefit from it. The teacher changed her attitude towards Peter once the diagnosis had been communicated to her and began to encourage and praise him for the slightest sign of effort.

The parents had accepted that in their opinion he would never achieve very much but when they began to see these signs of progress they also adopted a more positive, encouraging attitude and the whole situation snow-balled positively. Special school was no longer considered to be a viable option.

Overt aggression and bullying

Thomas was in Year 2 of secondary school. His academic record had always been poor although he had always excelled on the sportsfield. He was a natural footballer, being strong, fast and well co-ordinated. He made no secret of the fact that he was aiming one day to become a professional footballer. One might have expected him to have been popular with other boys in view of this sporting talent. Unfortunately, he was a bully and most children were afraid of him. In class he was often sullen and rude to teachers and was often on report.

Events came to a head on the day he physically attacked a teacher. The teacher in question had arrived at the classroom to find uproar and Thomas banging the head of a smaller boy against the wall. The teacher tried to intervene only to receive a violent blow on the arm himself. Fortunately the teacher wisely recognized that Thomas had lost control of himself so left the room for aid. He returned a few minutes later accompanied by the deputy head of the school only to find the class quiet and Thomas apparently reading a book.

Subsequently a psychological interview was arranged with the school psychologist. It was revealed that Thomas was virtually illiterate with a reading age of only 8 years and of very low self-esteem despite his footballing talents. The parents were also seen and a history taken. Thomas had suffered prolonged absence in the primary school owing to illnesses and had fallen behind in the basic school subjects as a result.

Remedial reading had been arranged from time to time but he had never really benefited from this. The parents were co-operative but were dismayed and surprised to learn of his reading retardation. Apparently he had always been inclined to be moody at home whenever school was imminent.

This case illustrates that for some children remedial reading is not sufficient in itself. Thomas was a typical case where a change in attitude needed to occur before he was able to benefit from the reading instruction. His low self-esteem prevented him from believing he was capable of learning, and no positive reinforcement could help him on that first rung of the ladder of success.

The case also illustrates how low self-esteem results from an area which is regarded as important by the significant people in a person's life. In Thomas's case it was reading failure. It also illustrates how success in a particular area does not necessarily compensate for low self-esteem in other areas. Academic success is the main focus of most schools and self-esteem comes from that area mainly.

In his case success on the football field was not valued very highly even though he loved it. If Thomas had not been a bully it is possible that he might have been able to compensate to some degree by receiving positive feedback from his peers with regard to his footballing ability. As things stood he received no positive feedback in any direction. Even his parents did not value his football as they were not interested in sport themselves.

Treatment

Once again a caring, totally accepting relationship needed to be established before Thomas could be helped. The teacher was, as is so often the case, far too busy and committed in other directions to take on this task but fortunately the school psychologist was able to do it. Eventually Thomas was able to take responsibility for his behaviour and to make an effort to change it.

At the same time a further attempt was made to provide remedial reading. This time it was organized within a self-concept theory framework, that is, self-initiation and self-checking games were used with the aid of a computer so that Thomas did not have to worry about being seen to fail in front of others. His motivation was much greater this time and soon he began to make progress. Reading materials concerned with football were provided when possible.

The following year his football ability came to the notice of the local association outside school and his self-esteem began to rise as his talent became more widely known and more genuinely admired by his parents, teachers and eventually by his peers.

The school refuser

Sometimes a pupil has frequent absences from school for no known reason. In desperation the parents seek medical opinion and are dismayed to be told that the cause is psychological. The child becomes anxious when having to face attendance at school. These cases have traditionally been known as 'school phobics', although this is probably a misnomer as most schools these days are pleasant places in which to work. The term *school refuser* is therefore to be preferred.

Derek was 6 years of age and had been attending school for only one year, but during that time had achieved only 40 per cent attendance. Usually his mother had supplied a medical certificate stating that her son was suffering from either migraine or stomach ache. Eventually the GP suggested a visit to the psychologist. He had noticed that Derek's problems appeared only when school was imminent.

The psychological examination revealed a very close-knit family and with Derek the only child. Although born prematurely and for a time a sickly child, he was now healthy and had no health problems apart from these regular headaches and stomach aches at school times.

The mother was described as overanxious. She continued to worry about Derek's health despite reassurance that he was a healthy boy. Whenever Derek felt he had a headache the mother confessed to worrying in case he had a serious illness and she herself ended up with a headache. The father was concerned but took a rather passive role in the family preferring to leave decisions to his wife. He idolized Derek, who could do no wrong in his eyes. There was little doubt that both parents had met Derek's every need from birth and he had no demands made on him at all.

The irregular school attendance had begun when Derek had complained to his mother that another child in his class had hit him and given him a headache. Without enquiring further his mother had suggested he stay away from school that day until he felt better. Derek jumped at the suggestion and so the pattern of absences begin. He had learned that to avoid school he had to have a headache. When he was persuaded to return he developed genuine aches and pains through anxiety.

It is a well established phenomenon that by avoiding a fearful situation it can be blown up in the imagination out of all proportion to the original event. When forced to attend school he found it stressful to have to share the teacher's attention with 25 other children. It was clear that this boy had received feedback at home which told him he was 'the most important person in the world' as a result of which he had developed a most unrealistic self-image.

This case illustrates the point made in Chapter 1 that we all feel secure behaving in ways which fit in with our image of ourselves. In this case Derek was not able to behave at school as if he was the most important person in the world. Consequently he felt anxious and insecure. Some degree of dissonance is inevitable as the two situations are different and most children quickly accommodate and integrate the new experiences of school into their developing self-images. In cases such as Derek's the contrast between home and school was far too radical for easy assimilation.

Treatment

The main focus on treatment was helping Derek achieve a realistic self-image. To enable this to happen meant enlisting the cooperation of both the teacher and the parents. The teacher was asked to give Derek a little extra attention while the parents, in comparison with their previous treatment of the boy, were asked to make more demands on him. The mother required lengthy counselling to help her do this and also to help her prepare to use firmness in getting Derek to school as even though co-operation had been promised Derek was still going to have to face up to that first attendance.

As predicted he threw a temper outburst; his parents remained calm but firm and Derek calmed down as soon as he was bundled into the classroom and his teacher welcomed him. Within one month he was a regular, happy member of the class, and his parents reported him a different boy at home.

From the examples quoted it can be seen how self-concept theory can often be a useful framework to the resolving of behaviour difficulties. An assumption is that in addition the teacher is of high self-esteem to be able to withstand the stresses involved in coping with behavioural difficulties. That topic is discussed in Chapter 8.

Further reading

Charles, C. (1995) *Building Classroom Discipline*. Longman, Harlow.

Gray, P., Miller, A., Nockes, J. (eds.) (1994) *Challenging Behaviour In Schools*. Routledge, London.

Haigh, G. (1994) *Managing Classroom Problems In The Primary School*. Paul Chapman Publishing, London.

Merrett, F. and Wheldall, K. (1990) *Positive Teaching in the Primary School*, Paul Chapman Publishing, London.

Chapter 7

Remedial reading

The research discussed in Appendix 1 arose as a result of my experience following several years of working in psychological and remedial departments and was conceived as an investigation into practical ways of helping students who are retarded in reading based on a self-concept theory approach.

The research began as an investigation into possible differences between students who score highly on reading tests and those who showed at least two years' retardation on the same tests. It was hypothesized that there would be differences in personal adjustment and the Cattell personality questionnaire was administered to a random sample of good readers and also to a random sample of poor readers. A statistical significance was observed between the two groups on the 'O' factor which Cattell describes as 'the extent to which the individual feels guilty about himself . . . it is a crude measure of self-image' (Lawrence, 1971).

Research findings

As a result of this finding the experiments described were set up with the hypothesis that students' reading attainment would rise if they could be helped to feel less guilty about themselves, that is, improve their self-esteem. This hypothesis was subsequently verified as described in Appendix 1.

From these experiments it looked as if self-esteem was causative over attainments, and over the years different researchers have argued about which comes first. The present conclusion seems to be that the relationship between reading attainment and self-esteem is a reciprocal one with each affecting the other. In practice, therefore, a dual approach should be used in most instances. In a small number of cases, however, it is not possible to help the student achieve success with a skill approach until he/she has had a change of self-concept. For these students a period of self-esteem enhancement through various activities is required before going on to introduce reading skills.

It is significant that whatever the type of provision or the level of expertise of the teacher, the kind of help given usually differs from what the child has already been receiving only to the extent that it is possible to give more individual attention. There continues to be a direct attack on the reading skills.

When children continue to fail despite remedial provision, the teacher often assumes that he/she has failed also – failed to find the right method or the best materials. The search then begins for different materials and methods. The suggestion that the reason for the child's failure may lie in his/her low level of self-esteem and that a primarily therapeutic approach might be more successful is rarely, if ever, considered. Although teachers may recognize the child's need for emotional attention as well as for the more obvious need to teach the skills of reading, beyond providing an atmosphere of encouragement, there is rarely an attempt to focus attention specifically on the child's self-concept. To concentrate on enhancing self-esteem would be an unusual occurrence to say the least. In my experience whenever it has been suggested that the teacher do this, the response has been one of surprise that a teacher might 'just talk' with the child when he/she so obviously needs to improve his/her reading skills.

The comment has been made that the DFEE would be upset if they 'merely chatted' with these children instead of teaching them. It is sad that the view still seems to be prevalent among many educational administrators as well as amongst some teachers that teaching is all about the purveying of knowledge. The fact that teachers have a grave responsibility for the development of the personalities of the children in their care seems to escape many of them. The view has sometimes been expressed to me that the home is the place for emotional development and the school for learning skills.

The results of the investigation reported in this book would suggest that teachers can do both – enhance self-esteem and also improve reading skills. It is somewhat daunting, however, to reflect on the fact that almost 40 years ago previous research was suggesting similar things, that is, that teachers who make warm accepting relationships with their pupils, avoiding negative and sarcastic comments, are those who in turn influence pupils' personality and attainments most (Perkin, 1958; Staines, 1958). Yet, 40 years on, many teachers still fail to appreciate the full significance of this kind of relationship.

For instance, there is still the tendency to demand more effort from the failing child when reference to the work of psychologists such as Rogers (1951) might help them to appreciate that sometimes the children who are failing in reading and seem to be avoiding it may be behaving simply according to their perception of themselves. In Rogers' view, 'Behaviour is basically the goal-directed attempt of the organism to satisfy its needs as experienced in the field as perceived'.

In the case of failing children, they see themselves as non-readers and so tend to avoid reading matter according to their perception of themselves. Whilst the teacher may see them as *potentially improving* readers, they see themselves as *permanently retarded* readers. Their perception of themselves as failing readers has become part of their 'internal frame of reference' (Rogers, 1951).

Motivation and reinforcement

It is clear from the work of Rogers and others in the phenomenological schools of psychology that the self-concept is a motivator. People tend to behave in ways which fit in with their perceptions of themselves. (This is discussed further in Chapter 1.) Those teachers who ignore self-concept theory will continue to focus on the pure skills approach and will also continue to find some students who do not make progress. The view has been expressed that all children can learn by breaking down the material to be learned into sufficiently small units and providing suitable reinforcement of behaviour (Skinner, 1953). In my experience and that of several remedial colleagues in practice it is not always possible to do this. In the first place some students are not attracted to any obvious reinforcer. It becomes impossible, therefore, to get these students on the first rung of that ladder of success.

Even when it may be possible to find a suitable reinforcer and learning does take place, these students do not always retain the material for very long. This can be so baffling to the teacher and there is a tendency to dismiss it with the explanation that the student has a 'poor memory'. A more likely explanation could lie within the *locus of control* construct which is discussed in Chapter 4. According to this view the student would need to believe that his/her own action was instrumental in receiving the reinforcer (Rotter, 1954). Those designated as 'externally controlled' do not believe that they are responsible for what happens to them. In other words, there is evidence from the work in the locus of control area that a reinforcer may not be sufficient in itself to produce a change in behaviour which lasts.

Therapeutic approaches

For many students retarded in reading a concentration early in the programme on reading skills gives confidence as they do indeed learn. These are the students whose reading difficulties are not usually of long standing and are not usually associated with any serious emotional problems. Quick success for them soon sets up the happy circle of improved reading and self-esteem (Figure 7.1).

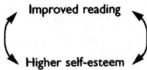

Figure 7.1   The happy circle

To organize a therapeutic approach for these children might produce an enjoyable experience for them, but it might be seen as wasting valuable time and resources which could be spent more profitably on children more obviously in need of therapy.

The problem of deciding which are the children in need of therapy and which do not need it should be resolved ideally during an initial diagnosis before treatment begins. However, it would be a costly exercise to refer all cases of reading retardation to a specialist such as an educational psychologist. Perhaps this is one reason why education departments usually operate on the principle that the majority of retarded readers will respond to a skills approach with a remedial teacher providing the necessary input.

It is only when these children do not respond to this approach that an educational psychologist would be asked to see the child. Normally this would be the first attempt to investigate possible emotional causes of the reading failure. A planned programme of help would be drawn up on the basis of this investigation which may involve both parents and children in therapy. Although at this stage there is recognition that emotional factors may have an important part to play in the problem it would be rare for the recommendation for treatment to involve counselling or drama as self-esteem enhancement. In my experience this has *never* happened.

There continues to be an emphasis on the skill acquisition usually through the organization of a more structured programme often with operant conditioning as its basis. The possible emotional factors receive attention through regular meetings between the child and the psychologist with the aim of helping the child resolve possible emotional conflicts or anxieties. Whilst in some cases this can be an effective means of helping, it is time-consuming, costly, and more important from the child's point of view, perhaps not even necessary.

Certainly, the results from the experiments reported in Appendix 1 would suggest other, less costly and perhaps more effective ways of helping most children retarded in reading. This would involve the establishment of a therapeutic programme in the school for the purpose of self-esteem enhancement. Only those children who did not respond to this programme would need the more skilled help of the educational psychologist. Although the experimental results clearly support the philosophy of therapeutic treatment, which treatment to use depends on the organization of the school as well as on the children.

For instance, the results suggest that some children do better through drama than through counselling. Those initially of lower self-esteem would appear to benefit more through drama whilst those of initially higher self-esteem would appear to respond slightly better to counselling. However, as discussed previously, the differences between these treatments is greater for children of higher self-esteem than for those of lower self-esteem. This means that whereas those of higher self-esteem should certainly be given counselling, the decision whether to give counselling or drama is not so critical for the lower self-esteem children.

Although the lower self-esteem children do slightly better with drama than with counselling the effects of the difference between these treatments is small. In practice, therefore, it might be more expedient to give them all counselling. In fact, it would be sensible to do this for all the children who had not made progress with the usual skills approach, once time and effort had gone into setting up counselling for the others.

On the other hand, there may be times when it would not be worth the expense and effort to organize counselling; particularly if the school already has an emphasis on drama in the normal curriculum. Only the particular self-esteem orientation and perhaps the content of the drama would need to be specially organized. In other words, the choice of counselling or drama as a therapeutic treatment would depend mainly on the exigencies of the school concerned.

It should also be borne in mind that the results of the experiment suggest additional advantages which accrue from the different treatments in terms of enhanced self-esteem and a shift towards internality on the locus of control dimension. However, it was reading attainment which was the main focus of attention in these experiments and which presumably would also be the main focus of attention for the remedial teacher.

Selecting appropriate treatment

Although the decision over which treatment to apply in a given case will depend mainly as stated on the school involved, it is important to emphasize that it should match the child. As an aid to this matching process the sequence model in Figure 7.2, based on the results of the main experiment, is suggested.

To understand the model it would help teachers to be aware of the different categories into which retarded readers fall. A child may have a difficulty in one or in several of these areas.

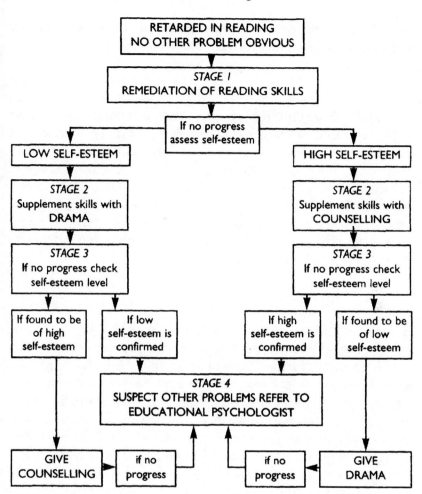

Figure 7.2 Processing sequence for retarded readers

Assuming that there are no obvious physical or sensory disabilities four stages of processing are recommended.

Stage 1

Stage 1 would show a concentration on remediating skills of reading, and it is hypothesized that the majority of retarded readers would be helped at this stage. They would be children whose reading difficulties are not of long standing and not normally associated with other problems. These children usually achieve quick success as discussed earlier. Those who do not respond to this treatment would fall into Stage 2.

Stage 2

At Stage 2, those children who made no progress using the pure skills approach of Stage 1 should receive therapeutic treatment in addition to further help with reading skills. It is suggested that counselling be organized for the high self-esteem children as was used successfully in the main experiment. Drama should be used, if the children had been identified as of particularly low self-esteem. However, as discussed earlier, the type of therapeutic treatment – counselling or drama – would depend largely on the exigencies of the school.

Stage 3

Stage 3 would be for those children left who have not made progress despite having gone through the previous stages. They would require further investigation into their level of self-esteem as some might easily be those referred to by Byrne (1961) as 'repressors'. In other words, those who had seemed to be of high self-esteem may have been repressing their 'true' self-esteem and would really be of low self-esteem. If, indeed, they had been repressing their low self-esteem and were really of low self-esteem, then they should be given drama. There may also be children in this group who were wrongly assessed as being of low self-esteem. These children should be given counselling.

Stage 4

Stage 4 would be concerned with those children who have not responded well to any of the other approaches. They would be in a small minority and should be referred to an educational psychologist for a more skilled assessment and treatment. Those with severe emotional and social difficulties and/or possible physical or sensory difficulties would come into this category. It is likely that they would be showing overt signs of their emotional difficulties through difficult behaviour in the classroom.

Clearly, it is Stage 3 which is the focus of interest with its processing of therapeutic treatments, and for which the experimental results provided evidence.

The maintenance of reading gains in the long term

The question of the effectiveness of remedial education has over the years proved to be a controversial issue. There have been those who have written of its undoubted value and also those who have cast doubt on its long-term effectiveness (Collins, 1961; Chazan, 1967; Cashdan and Pumfrey, 1969). This is debated at some length in the Bullock Report (1975) which points out the conflicting evidence, and also the difficulties involved in evaluating the various remedial provision.

Remedial education means different things to different workers; the criteria for selecting the children are variable; and types of provision vary between education authorities. Despite this difficulty of being able to evaluate the remedial work writers continue to argue over its effectiveness. Whatever the conclusions it is interesting and significant to note that the research is notable for its lack of attention to the self-concept.

It is strongly advocated here that before conclusions are drawn with any real validity attempts should have been made in the research to focus on the student's self-concept, and it is suggested that long-term gains would be made only where there has been a corresponding change in the self-concept. It is only through a change in the student's perception of him/herself that the student will begin to perceive him/herself as a good reader and, therefore, only with this will come the motivation to seek out reading matter independently and in so doing rehearse what has been learned. Without this corresponding change in the self-concept the student will merely have learned to perform a few tricks with words. The motivation to seek out further reading will not be there. He/she will continue with his/her former attitudes towards reading and have the attitude that 'it is not me'. Once able to perceive him/herself differently he/she will be more inclined to seek further reading experiences outside the remedial lesson.

Without a change of self-concept, any improvements made during remedial lessons are not necessarily perceived as signifi-

84 *Enhancing Self-Esteem*

cant to the student – as part of his/her self-concept. Although having pleased the teacher by learning additional skills, away from the teacher these students continue to perceive themselves as poor readers and will quickly revert to their former state of reading inadequacy. So it is not surprising to discover in various studies that long-term gains were negligible.

The effects of therapeutic intervention on dyslexic students

Dyslexia is a term used to describe children who have a specific difficulty in learning literacy skills, as opposed to those who are seen to have an all-round general learning difficulty. Arguments over the usefulness of this term continue to fill the pages of journals and books. There are those on the one hand who deny the concept altogether while at the other extreme there are those who stoutly maintain that there is a group of children who have specific learning difficulties, usually in the area of working memory, which require specialist help. Most researchers in this area would concur with the view that some children indeed do have specific learning difficulties which inevitably cause them problems in learning to read and to spell properly.

It is interesting that in the experiments described in Chapter 2 no attempt was made to screen children for dyslexia. Surveys of the numbers of children who could be considered to fall into the dyslexic category vary from 4 per cent in British surveys (Miles and Haslum, 1986) to 25 per cent in American surveys (Farnham-Diggory, 1978). If one accepts these figures undoubtedly there would have been a not inconsiderable number of dyslexic children amongst those in the experimental groups. Some of these children may have contributed to the 'within group' errors.

Any dyslexic children presumably would have been distributed randomly over the four treatment groups and if they had been excluded from the final statistical analysis it is probable that the differences between the treatment would have been even more marked.

Children with specific learning difficulties, known as dyslexia, are likely to present a special case of low self-esteem unless identified early. The research would suggest that a specific learning difficulty of this sort can last throughout life and without a thorough psychological assessment teachers are not going to know how best to help the children cope with the problems and perhaps how to compensate for them. Low self-esteem can soon develop under these circumstances.

The bright child who has not had a cognitive assessment identifying the precise nature of his/her difficulties would experience particular frustration. This child is often well able to contribute intelligently in oral lessons, easily capable of understanding the import of the discussion but unable to read or write about it without some considerable effort. Anthony (1968), in a study of children with symptoms of dyslexia, referred to a 'global stress' factor which he described as limiting the children's capacity to cope. Whilst this observation would probably apply not only to dyslexics but also to most children with learning difficulties, once again it highlights the relationship between low self-esteem and literacy skills. Children who feel unable to cope are certainly at risk of developing low self-esteem.

It is possible that the extent to which a learning disability results in a handicapping condition depends on the level of self-esteem. Some children who are dyslexic may have learned to cope and so maintain their self-esteem by concentrating on their strengths. An accurate cognitive profile identifying strengths and weaknesses in the child is essential in knowing how best to teach children with reading difficulties whether categorized as dyslexic or otherwise.

Further reading

Brown E.N. (1990) Children with spelling and writing difficulties: an alternative approach in Pumphrey, P. and Elliott, C. (eds.) *Children's Difficulties in Reading, Spelling and Writing*. Lewes, Falmer.

Bryant, P. and Bradley, L. (1985) *Children's Reading Problems*. Oxford, Blackwell.

Pumphrey, P. D. and Reason, R. (1991) *Specific Learning Difficulties (Dyslexia), Challenges and Responses*. Windsor, NFER-Nelson.

Chapter 8

The teacher's self-esteem

Reference is made in previous chapters to the influence of teachers' own self-esteem. There is clear evidence to show that without teachers themselves being confident and having high self-esteem they are not easily going to be able to enhance the self-esteem of the children in their care. So what can teachers do to ensure their own high self-esteem?

The bookstalls and popular press have always had 'experts' of one kind or another giving advice on how to 'feel more confident', how to 'lead a fuller life', how to 'feel in control of your life', and so on. The trouble with popular advice of this kind is that it is rarely based on sound theoretical bases, and more often than not simply exhorts people 'to think positive'. Whilst this is admirable advice it is only part of the story. To enhance your own self-esteem it is desirable, first, to be aware of the theoretical background of self-concept as outlined in earlier chapters. Secondly, it requires a belief in the hedonistic philosophy which may be difficult for some teachers to accept. Thirdly, it requires commitment to the belief that we all have the power for change within ourselves. This means that we are potentially capable of being self-determinate, often despite unfortunate backgrounds. Lastly, it means being able to accept and value the 'inner self' and to be able to distinguish it from the 'outward behaviour'. Let us deal with each of these in turn, assuming first that the teacher has read the earlier chapters and so is familiar with self-concept theory.

The hedonistic philosophy

There are probably more philosophies of life than there are theories in psychology, the most common being those of a religious flavour and concerned with giving help to others. However, one important aspect of these philosophies of helping others, which tends to receive scant attention, is that before we can effectively have regard for others we need to have regard for ourselves. The phrase 'Charity begins at home' is so apt here. We are more likely to like others if we first like ourselves. Unfortunately liking yourself is not always easy especially once the low self-esteem process has begun. Indeed, the view is sometimes expressed that giving too much attention to our own needs is selfish and therefore undesirable.

The hedonistic philosophy implies that the giving expression to our own needs is essential to self-esteem enhancement, but this does not mean expressing them with no regard for the feelings of others. It emphasizes the social nature of humanity. It emphasizes that life is meant to be enjoyed and does not agree with the view that goodness only exists through denial. It means that we should take stock of our lifestyle and ask whether we are receiving job satisfaction.

Teaching is inherently demanding and job satisfaction can quickly be reduced through factors such as 'role ambiguity', difficult staff relations, coping with difficult children. All these have been identified by researchers as common sources of stress in teaching (Pratt, 1978). Job overload and role ambiguity have increased over the last two decades as countless changes in education have been forced upon schools. This has resulted in an inevitable rise in teacher stress. Prolonged stress and reduced job satisfaction will produce feelings of inadequacy and so low self-esteem in the teacher. Sources of stress such as those identified as common should be removed as far as possible before they result in low self-esteem.

If a teacher is not enjoying school then efforts should be made to identify the sources of stress and remove the barriers to satisfaction. It is not justified to adopt the view that teaching has inevitably to be stressful or that it is 'character-building' to suffer stress. Although there will be aspects of school life which are sometimes unpleasant they should not be accepted as inevitable. A hedonistic philosophy does not mean an acceptance of adverse circumstances. It is an active philosophy which focuses on the need to work at producing a more enjoyable lifestyle.

There are some sources of stress in teaching which are not within the power of the teacher to change, for example, the relationship with the school head and the administration. Providing, however, that the teacher controls those factors which are controllable and has begun to develop high self-esteem these other factors will cease to have potency. High self-esteem in all of us has the effect of increasing our coping capacities.

The question is rightly: Just how can the teacher set about developing high self-esteem and so increase his/her capacity to cope with the inevitable stressors of change? The evidence from clinical work and from the humanistic school of psychology in particular shows that it is perfectly possible for people to change their behaviour and their emotions if they are sufficiently motivated and prepared to make the necessary effort to do so. The remainder of this chapter is devoted to showing teachers how to maintain their self-esteem and so reduce the effects of stress.

Changing emotions by changing thinking

It is a mistake to think that we are all prisoners of our early experiences. The classical Freudian view implies that our inadequacies are so often relics of our childhood days and to remove their effects it is necessary to relive these early experiences. It is now generally accepted that this view is extreme and that it is possible to resolve present difficulties and to change present attitudes without always needing to 'unravel the past'. The evidence points to the view that people are motivated not only by their past experiences but also by their anticipation of the future. We are all able to change if we wish to do so and are prepared for the effort. How do we set about doing this?

Events themselves do not cause emotions. Emotions are caused by our interpretation of events. Following this line of reasoning it becomes clear that it is possible to change emotions by thinking in a particular way. This 'rational-emotive' approach to behaviour forms the basis of the theories of Albert Ellis (1979). Although his theories are more usually encountered in psychotherapy they also have something to offer teachers and others who may find themselves under stress. The following scene illustrates this and describes the steps to go through when setting out to reduce stress by changing thinking.

Scene

A teacher feels inadequate because of regularly troublesome behaviour of two pupils in her class. These pupils disrupt lessons and seem impervious to any approach. The teacher goes home at the end of each day exhausted and with feelings of failure.

Strategy

The situation should be clearly analysed under the three headings of 'thinking–feeling–action'.

Step 1: Analysis of feelings at time of stress. Possible answer: 'I felt angry, silly and humiliated.'

Step 2: Analysis of thinking at time of stress. Possible answer: 'I am no good as a teacher. The children do not like me.' This step is often difficult for people. They may say, 'I wasn't thinking of anything. I was too angry at the time'. The very fact of being forced to trace the origins of the emotions and to be able to put these emotions into words is the essence of the rational-emotive approach. So no matter how difficult it may seem, it is important that the thinking is recalled and analysed.

Step 3: Analysis of behaviour at the time of the stress. Possible answer: 'I shouted and clenched my fists.'

Step 4: Go through the following relaxation procedure:

- Sit in a comfortable chair which supports the head.
- Focus on a point on the ceiling until the eyes become tired and begin to blink.
- Close the eyes as it becomes unpleasant to leave them open.
- Think of each muscle and joint in the body in turn beginning with the ankles.
- While doing this say the word 'relax' as you move to the next one.
- Focus particularly on the stomach muscles.
- Conclude by relaxing the facial muscles and even the tongue.
- Now observe the breathing remembering that it is automatic.
- Let 'it' breathe as and when 'it' wants to.
- With every breath out say the word 'relax'.
- Repeat this 10 times.

Step 5: Visualize yourself as a successful teacher, smiling and with a happy contented class:

- See in your mind's eye the troublesome pupils and visualize them behaving properly.
- Talk to yourself, saying positive things about yourself changing those words used when under stress and substituting them for positive ones, e.g. 'I get on well with the other pupils and they like me. I know I am becoming a better teacher every day'.

It is important to visualize the scene in addition to changing your thinking as the aim is to 'condition the unconscious mind' which operates in pictures.

Step 6: Deliberately seek out the stressful situation in real life and as soon as the feelings of stress make their appearance say quietly to yourself the word 'relax'. Immediately the body will begin to assume a relaxed mode. On the first occasion after having gone through the procedure only a slight change will be experienced. With regular practice, however, a permanent change will occur. The relaxation and visualization should be practised once a day until the situation is no longer felt to be stressful. This would normally take no longer than a fortnight.

One example of a stressful teacher could be someone who worries over not getting on with other teachers in the staffroom. This is common, as the research into sources of teacher stress indicates. The teacher would need to translate this worry into specific behaviour and as a result may discover that other teachers do not talk to him/her very much. The next step would be to ask him/herself why this is so. The answer invariably would be that there is something wrong with the others. Whilst this may be so, to blame others does not solve the problem.

The teacher must always ask him/herself 'What is it in me that results in this behaviour?' The answer could be that the teacher has developed the habit now of avoiding or ignoring social contact. In that case the desired behaviour change would be to practise making friendly overtures and initiating conversations. The teacher may say 'He/she made me angry'. This is not the case in actual fact. The teacher made him/herself angry.

Think positive

It is all too easy for teachers to fall into the habit of negative thinking, particularly if having to deal with difficult behaviour in children. They also tend to be unduly critical of themselves and blame themselves for not being able to deal with the behaviour. An interesting experiment was devised by Hannum (1974) to help teachers become less critical. Hannum set out to help two teachers become less self-critical. The aim was to increase their positive thoughts about themselves and to decrease their negative self-thoughts. They were asked to make wrist counts of their thoughts and observers in the classroom noted their negative and positive behaviours towards the students. Following a baseline period, they were asked to say deliberately 'stop' whenever they felt a negative thought coming on. There was a gradual increase in positive thoughts and also in positive behaviour towards the students. All that was required was for the teachers to make a conscious effort to change their negative set.

Self-acceptance

The required changes in our emotions and subsequently in behaviour do not always occur immediately and need regular practice. In the mean time it is essential that the teacher accepts the undesirable behaviour in him/herself until the changes are felt. This is where the principle of self-acceptance is important. This requires an attitude of acceptance of the possibility of change as discussed but, in addition, requires the ability to separate our behaviour from our 'inner self'. It is likely to need practice again as changes are being attempted from behaviour which is probably of long standing, and habit is a strong motivating factor in all behaviour. 'Self-acceptance' is similar to the principle discussed in Chapter 3 with regard to accepting the personality of the child even if not accepting the behaviour.

A beginning towards this self-acceptance is the process of affirmation. The following affirmations should be practised:

- 'I am a confident person.'
- 'I am a strong person.'
- 'I am a happy person.'
- 'My motives are always for the best.'
- 'I am improving in every way.'

Acceptance of inadequacies and/or failures should be practised by affirming the preceding and recognizing that even when the behaviour is sometimes not exactly what was desired or planned the inner self is still intact and is 'doing its best'. It is particularly important that this kind of attitude is practised following an unpleasant experience which my have resulted in feelings of inadequacy. Implicit in this affirmation is the belief in the separateness of the self.

We often tell ourselves 'we are no good' when we have had a personal failure. This statement is made when we have not separated our behaviour from our unique inner self. Once we can make this distinction we can appreciate the illogicality of saying 'I am no good' as a result of one unpleasant situation. We should say instead 'My behaviour was no good but I am still a strong, confident, happy person inside'. Next time perhaps the behaviour will not be so bad.

In other words, 'I like me even if I sometimes dislike what I do'. The adoption of this attitude will prevent the low self-esteem person from continually punishing him/herself and feeling guilty.

Difficult parents as a threat to self-esteem

The regular practising of the preceding principles should help reduce stress and so maintain the teacher's self-esteem but, in addition, it is also helpful to be prepared for situations which can be a threat to self-esteem. Amongst these is the difficult parent.

The chances are high that most teachers sooner or later will encounter a difficult parent. Usually this is as a result of an invitation from the teacher to discuss the child's behaviour or work. Less frequently it will be as a result of a difficult parent arriving at the school, often unannounced, to complain about the school's treatment of his/her child. Whether the parent arrives on his/her own initiative or through invitation, the situation is fraught with the potential for further difficulties. Whether or not these further difficulties subsequently appear is going to depend largely on the skill of the teacher in the area of interpersonal relationships.

Assessing and handling the aggressive parents

The starting point for handling a difficult parent is to try to see the situation from the parent's point of view. This means recognizing first that if the parent is there because of difficulties with the child, he/she is likely to feel inadequate and be on the defensive.

The manner in which parents of a difficult child will protect their self-esteem will vary along a continuum ranging from overtly aggressive to timid, withdrawn behaviour. Which is shown, depends on temperament. It seems that the more extroverted by temperament are inclined to be aggressive, whilst the more introverted in temperament are likely to be withdrawn and nervous. From the teacher's point of view, it is useful to know that whichever behaviour is shown, the chances are that it is an attempt to maintain self-esteem in the face of feelings of inadequacy. Once this is understood, the teacher is less likely to react with irritation or aggression, and so remains able to establish productive communication.

As a prelude to discussing the nature of the child's problem it is essential that the parents are helped to appreciate that the interview is non-threatening to their self-esteem. Once this has been communicated the interview should begin by inviting the parents to take a seat and by sitting alongside them without the barrier of a desk. The psychology of non-verbal behaviour tells us that an interview conducted from behind a desk conveys a message of superiority. As a further prelude, it is important to regard the problem as a 'problem situation' and not a 'problem child' or a 'problem parent'.

The aim should be not to apportion blame, but rather for teacher and parent to work together to try to resolve the difficult situation. Unfortunately, it is not enough to have this intention. Even when parents accept that the teacher is not an active threat to their self-esteem, they are still likely to find, on occasions, that they cannot get 'on the teacher's wavelength'. We have all had the experience of feeling that we are not being understood, and in the case of the difficult parent, already perhaps oversensitive to this need, it is essential for the teacher to be able to establish an empathic relationship. If this kind of relationship can be established quickly, the parent is more likely to trust the teacher and therefore to be more receptive to suggestions of change. Unfortunately, empathy is not always easy to achieve.

Obviously it will be easier if the parents and teacher come from similar socioeconomic backgrounds. The more alike they are the more they will understand the other's point of view. This is just the beginning of the establishment of an empathic relationship. Equally important is the ability to listen.

Listening means more than just hearing verbal utterances. It means also, in this context, being able to hear the feelings behind the words. This is a skill many people seem to possess naturally, but it can always be trained. It involves being able to reflect the feelings once they have been perceived, for example, if the parent should say 'I don't know what to do to make my son work', the teacher should try to understand what the parent is feeling when the statement is made. It is possible for many feelings to be expressed. If the feeling seems to be 'I feel helpless' then the teacher might reflect this feeling, for example, 'You sound as if you feel helpless in this situation'.

In addition to the reflection of feeling, another skill as an aid to empathy is the capacity for revealing one's own personality. It helps, for instance, if the teacher can communicate that he/she has met that problem before. 'I know what you mean, my child was the same'. So much the better, of course, if this can be followed up with a comment that eventually the difficulties were resolved.

In summary, the following sequence of events should be followed:

1. Welcome the parents and communicate acceptance.
2. Allow the parents time to express their feelings without criticism.
3. Emphasize the 'problem situation' and not the 'problem child'.
4. Try to show genuineness and empathy throughout the interview.

Dealing with self-esteem threat

So far we have looked at the aggressive parent. A slightly different problem are the parents who complain that their child is not achieving as highly as they wish. It is important that the same principles as already discussed are maintained, but in this case it is easier for the teacher to begin to feel inadequate. To be accused by an intelligent articulate parent of being a poor teacher is almost calculated to result in feelings of aggression, or in feelings of insecurity and inadequacy. However, if the teacher is prepared for this reaction he/she will handle it better.

If teachers recognize that any professional is at risk in this way, then they will not over-react. The question is: Why should teachers feel threatened by such accusations? In the first place, we all need to be liked and to receive approval. If our competence is threatened our immediate reaction is normally to feel disappointment. This feeling is then usually replaced by indignation. It may stop there, particularly if the teacher knows that the parent's accusations are unfounded. However, it is not always easy in education to be sure that what we do is always responsible for the outcomes. More often than not, therefore, the teacher who is unprepared is going to be a prey to undesirable emotions. What can be done about them?

As already indicated, a strong self-concept is more likely to be able to cope with these feelings. This means a person who is doing a satisfying job and is confident that he/she is doing it well. A strong self-concept means being able to communicate easily and to be spontaneous in emotional expression. It means above all having a knowledge of one's own personality. This means that when feelings of irritation or feelings of insecurity ensue, reason will prevail. It will be possible to listen to the parent's accusations objectively without over-reacting. Unfortunately, not all of us have this kind of strength.

For most of us, perhaps, an attack on our professional competence is a threat to our self-esteem. Once we experience this threat we should immediately ask ourselves 'What is it in me which causes me to feel like this?' This question will have the main purpose of reminding the teacher that the feeling indeed originates from within and is not something imposed from the parent. It will also have the purpose of causing the teacher to think before acting adversely. It is a bit like 'counting to 10' before saying something when angry. It should then be possible to begin the negotiation with the relationship still intact and without the teacher feeling loss of self-esteem.

Teachers who recognize their lack of assertion need not be discouraged as there is plenty of evidence to illustrate that with practice they can become gradually more assertive. The key phrase here is 'with practice'. The importance of being prepared cannot be overemphasized, so that the very words to be used have been rehearsed. Thomas Gordon (1974) has shown how the use of the three words 'I', 'when' and 'because' are the key to successful communication in this context. Although Gordon was advocating using this formula with children the same principles apply when communicating assertively with another adult. The following sentences illustrate:

- 'I feel upset when people do that because I cannot hear myself speak.'
- 'I feel angry when I'm interrupted because it seems that my opinion does not count.'
- 'I become embarrassed when asked to do that because I feel undervalued.'

The main point is that feelings are communicated without fear and also a reason for them is given.

Be organized

Insecurities and stress can come from not having planned the day properly. Teachers know full well the importance of planning lessons but how many have made a plan for the whole day, including after school? It seems to be a natural phenomenon for human beings to 'know where they stand'. Nature abhors a vacuum and it is a source of comfort to know what is to be expected. Ambiguities are a common source of stress. It is suggested that teachers begin each day with the motto: 'Plan for the day', not just 'Plan for the teaching'.

Before arriving at school teachers should

- make a list of 'jobs for the day' in order of their importance; and
- estimate the time required for each job.

During free time at school teachers should

- make a list of 'jobs for the term';
- ensure privacy if necessary, e.g. close door and place on it 'Do Not Disturb';
- delegate jobs where possible; and
- spend five minutes just thinking about their role as a teacher.

Become an expert

The world seems to need experts. This is probably a reflection of the times in which we live. So if a teacher can develop a talent through a particular interest it usually has the effect of enhancing self-esteem as others notice the talent and admire it. The fascinating thing is that you do not need to be a real expert in the true sense of the word for this to happen, so great is the need for people to admire experts. Simply developing a reputation for being interested in a particular area, e.g. dyslexia, will cause others to regard you as the expert. This will cause the teacher's self-image to be changed and as the Self is a motivator this regard from others will cause the teacher to seek out information on dyslexia. Very soon the teacher will begin to know more about the subject than his/her colleagues. The lesson is for teachers to take an interest in a specialist area.

Have fun

Teaching can be a very serious job if we let it be so. It is not always easy to be lighthearted in the face of all the stresses which go with the job. The other side of the coin is that people who have a sense of humour and appear to have fun in their work usually have high self-esteem. So teachers should ensure that they maintain their sense of humour and deliberately ensure they do have fun when that is possible. By all means, take your work seriously, but never take yourself seriously to the extent that you lose your sense of humour! The lesson for us all is that we have to set about organizing our lives so that we do have a regular period set aside for having fun whether this be a night out in a restaurant or a night in watching a favourite TV programme.

Maintaining self-esteem as a manager

The management of a team in any organization should be based on sound management principles. Whilst this is a topic in its own right and one which can only be dealt with superficially at the risk of trivializing it, there is one aspect of team management which has to be addressed here. This is the problem of maintaining self-esteem while managing a team of teachers. Teachers are a group of professionals renowned for their individualism and managing them can present some considerable problems.

In general terms there are broadly three different styles of leadership – the *laissez-faire* type, where the leader is content to allow decisions to be made according to the whims of the group, the authoritarian, where the leader makes decisions without consulting the group, and finally the democratic leader, where decisions are made with group consultation. Not surprisingly, it is the democratic style of leadership which is judged to be the most effective in maintaining self-esteem and group morale. The other two leadership styles, as well as being bad for group morale, also tend to produce hostility in a group.

In Chapter 3 mention was made of those desirable qualities of personality which make for effective communicators – empathy, genuineness and acceptance. These same qualities of course are essential in a team manager. They are particularly important when the manager has to make demands on others which they may have difficulty in accepting. The democratic manager who possesses these qualities will also have high self-esteem and be able to be assertive. Demands will then be made through a process of negotiation using 'I' messages and active listening (empathy) as illustrated in the following dramatic scene. This formula can also be considered as a four-step method for resolving conflict as follows:

- *Step 1*: Both parties express their needs using active listening with 'I' messages.
- *Step 2*: Active listening (empathy) is used to consider possible solutions.
- *Step 3*: Alternative solutions are then considered without criticism.
- *Step 4*: A solution is agreed upon through consensus so nobody loses.

Resolving conflicts: a four-step method

- *Step 1: Both parties express their needs. Active listening is used along with 'I' messages.*
- *Step 2: Possible solutions are considered and active listening continues to be used.*
- *Step 3: Alternative solutions are considered without criticism.*
- *Step 4: A solution is adopted through consensus so nobody loses.*

Example

The headteacher has sent a note to the school caretaker asking him to prepare a room in the school and to have it open next Saturday for the first meeting of the school chess club. The caretaker has said that he cannot do this owing to another commitment. They meet.

Headteacher	I need the room prepared with adequate seating and to be open by 9 a.m. on Saturday because Saturdays are the only time we can get the students and their parents together ['I' messages].
Caretaker	I can't do it on Saturday. I have a family, you know.
Headteacher	It sounds as if you have made arrangements which are difficult to break [empathy].
Caretaker	Yes, I have, I've promised them I'd go camping with them next Saturday so I can't help.
Headteacher	You probably feel you would be letting them down if you had to cancel the camp. Is there any way around this do you think? [Step 2.]
Caretaker	Well, why not have the chess group during the week?
Headteacher	That sounds a good idea but the parents won't all be able to come during the week. How would it be if we had the meeting the following Saturday? [Step 3.]
Caretaker	I think I could manage that but I'd have to come back early from the camp.
Headteacher	OK. How about the Saturday after that one? [Step 4.]
Caretaker	Yes, that would be fine. No problems at all.

Example

The team manager has asked a particular teacher to take a group of school children along to a football match on a Saturday morning. Nobody wants to do this on their day off!

Manager	I need somebody to take the children to the game as I cannot go myself. They have all expressed disappointment at the thought of missing it and I do think they should see the game ['I' message].
Teacher	I can't go as I've promised to take my family to buy some new clothes this Saturday.
Manager	It sounds then as if you are already committed. [Empathy.]
Teacher	Yes, I'm afraid so. They have to have new things for their holiday next month.
Manager	So you feel you would be letting them down if you had to cancel their shopping [Empathy]. Is there any way around this, do you think? [Step 2.]
Teacher	Well, I could put the shopping off until another day but I just don't have the time, unless of course I could take some time off during school hours.
Manager	Taking time off sounds a possible solution but first have you thought of asking your husband to take your children shopping? [Step 3.]
Teacher	What! He is hopeless at that sort of thing. He would not know what to buy.
Manager	I see. Well supposing the head would agree to your taking time off, would that really be the answer to the problem?
Teacher	Well, yes, if the head agrees to my doing the shopping on Thursday morning then I could take the children to the game on Saturday as you have asked me to do.
Manager	Right! I'm sure the head would agree under the circumstances. [Step 4.]

Using the four-step method meant that there were no winners or losers in this conflict. The following principles were observed in this process:

• The manager made his needs known clearly by using 'I' messages.
• The teacher was given the opportunity to react to the messages.

- The manager used active listening, communicating understanding of the teacher's feelings.
- The teacher was given the opportunity to suggest possible solutions.
- A compromise solution was obtained through negotiation.

Accept your limitations

Teachers are generally known for being 'tender minded' and caring people. Whilst these are admirable qualities for people in the helping professions – and I would consider teaching to be a helping profession – they can place teachers at a disadvantage when having to cope with stress. An example of this is the common observation that teachers tend to blame themselves if the children in their care have problems. The teacher with the child who does not make progress in reading attainment asks him/herself why he/she cannot find the way through to help this child. The teacher with the child who is a discipline problem asks him/herself why he/she cannot control the class. Whilst this kind of introspective self-examination can lead to constructive action it can also become intropunitive and can generalize to the extent that the teacher ends up questioning his/her suitability for the job. It is important that teachers understand that all teachers are a prey to this kind of thinking and they need to be able to distance themselves from the child with the problem. With regard to academic attainments they should remind themselves that there will always be some children for whom progress is going to be slow. In the case of behavioural difficulties, there will always be some children who are so emotionally disturbed that they cannot be helped in the ordinary classroom. Teachers should not be afraid to admit that they may have a child whom they cannot control. It is sometimes thought to be a character defect if a teacher cannot control children. This is wrong. It cannot be sufficiently emphasized that controlling groups of children can be very difficult and is a skill which has to be learned. There are many well researched strategies which teachers can put into practice but teachers are not born knowing what they are! They need to be shown what to do! The first step is to accept they do have a problem in this area and then to request help either from a senior colleague, the local educational psychologist or apply to go on an in-service course.

Expressing pleasure at successes

Most teachers are modest people. This may be largely a cultural factor but it seems that people generally in Britain do not easily broadcast their achievements. Why should we not in the staffroom announce with pleasure that we have just been able to get a difficult child to read, or that we have just passed our latest examination? Perhaps it could be a routine procedure at the end of a staff meeting for the head to ask if anybody has any achievements or been known to have made a particular effort during the previous week they would like to announce. A refinement of this would be for the head to ask staff to let him/ her know before the staff meeting of any teachers who have experienced a notable success or been known to have made a big effort in some direction. A tangible recognition of this could then be presented to the appropriate teacher at the meeting followed by a round of applause from the others.

It is OK to change your mind

Some people regard changing their mind as a sign of weakness and will rigidly stick to a decision as a matter of principle. But circumstances sometimes change so that it becomes prudent to change your mind. It is OK to change your mind when there is a logical reason for doing so. A class rule should be changed, for instance, if the teacher has evidence that it is not working. To be able to be flexible is the mark of the high self-esteem person.

Take time to make decisions

We all tend to place a premium on making quick decisions. People are often pushed into doing so and are expected to make a decision on the spot. This is common at staff meetings when teachers do not want to be thought to be 'ditherers'. The fact is that it is not always easy to make a quick decision without some considerable thought. Where this is the case people should not be afraid to ask for time before responding.

Make your needs known

'Assertiveness training' has assumed a popularity these days amongst courses on 'self-development'. As there is a positive correlation between assertiveness and self-esteem all teachers need to be sure they are appropriately assertive. This does not mean being aggressive. Indeed, it is possible to rate yourself along a dimension of assertiveness from 'submissive' at one end of a scale to 'aggressive' at the other end. We should aim to be at the midpoint on this scale:

Submissive → Assertive → Aggressive

The submissive teacher would be unable to express controversial opinions at a staff meeting. These teachers tend to avoid unpleasant situations or conflict with others. The aggressive teacher would not be so reticent but would be inclined to express themselves in an unpleasant fashion, demanding others accept their views, and demanding their needs be satisfied. Assertive teachers are unafraid to say what they mean or what they want, expressing themselves politely but firmly. They are calm in their presentations and are ready to repeat their needs if necessary.

There is another type of teacher who may not be lacking in assertion so much as lacking the capacity to empathize with others. At a staff meeting, for instance, this kind of teacher would tend to assume that the others at the meeting know him/her well enough to be able to know what he/she wants or what he/she is thinking. The reality can be very different as people often see things in different ways and from different perspectives. This assumption can lead to disappointments and some degree of stress as after a meeting is over they realize their views have not been taken into account. We cannot always guarantee that others will automatically know what we want without our saying what it is. So it is important always to state our needs firmly but politely when decisions are being made which affect our welfare or our method of operation.

Self-esteem and teacher stress

No discussion on teacher self-esteem would be complete without mentioning teacher stress. The relationship between teacher stress and low self-esteem is part of a vicious circle as when teachers suffer from stress their self-esteem drops. This affects children's self-esteem which in turn affects their achievements and their behaviour. The circle continues with teachers being put under stress by difficult children, and so it goes on . . .

Whenever people suffer from stress their self-esteem is immediately put at risk. People feel guilty when they have to admit that they may not be able to cope with the demands of the job. Teaching is no exception to this. In fact the evidence points very firmly to the view that of all the professions teaching is potentially the most stressful. In a large survey conducted by Cox (1978), 70 per cent of teachers mentioned the job itself as their main source of stress. This was compared with only 38 per cent of people in other professions surveyed who considered the job to be their main source of stress. Admittedly this research took place almost 20 years ago but there are firm grounds for believing that today teacher stress is even more common. There is plenty of evidence to show that the very nature of the work done is conducive to stress amongst the most stable of teachers. The irony is that unless people have been teachers they can have little appreciation of this fact. To the outsider it appears to be a very congenial job indeed with its short hours and long holidays. To those who are teachers or have been teachers this is far from the truth.

Most research today points to job overload, difficult children and feelings of inadequacy as the sources of teacher stress with feelings of inadequacy more likely to be the end product than a main source of stress. In other words teachers are all at risk of suffering low self-esteem.

Definitions of stress vary but the one by McGrath (1970) is probably the one most easily recognized by teachers: 'a perceived substantial imbalance between demand and response capability, under conditions where failure to meet demand has important perceived consequences.' The consequences for teachers can range from irritability and headaches to the more serious nervous breakdown. From the point of view of teacher self-esteem, clearly, it is important first for teachers to recognize that they are at risk and then for them to learn strategies for coping with it.

All schools should try to arrange regular staff meetings in an informal, non-threatening setting where they would be encouraged to discuss problems faced in the classroom. This is commonly found in industry, sometimes with staff enjoying the luxury of an overnight stay in a first-class hotel. The starting point is first to accept that all teachers will have problems and not to feel it is some kind of character defect to have to admit it. Practical help can be given at these meetings by teachers having experienced the same kind of problems. Additionally, the emotional support experienced can be invaluable in combating stress.

The four-step method of stress management, devised by the author, is outlined below. This is a technique which has been described by some as 'self-hypnosis'. It is based on the following observations:

- Relaxation is incompatible with stress.
- It is possible to associate the word 'relax' with feelings of relaxation.

Teachers who wonder whether they may already be suffering from stress should complete the questionnaire in Figure 8.1.

Four-step method of stress management

Step 1: What you feel   Under this heading try to recall the precise feelings. It is essential you are accurate. For example, did you really feel panic or was it merely the milder feeling of apprehension? Once recalled the feelings should be written down.

Step 2: What you think   Write down the precise thoughts which go through your head when having the feelings. This is not always easy and people sometimes say 'I wasn't thinking anything; I was too scared' or whatever. Even if you are one of these people do persist until you do eventually identify the feelings.

Step 3: What you did   Write down what you did at the time of the stress, e.g. did you cry/run away, complain, etc.?

Step 4: The treatment stage First you should practise a relaxation technique. There are many different methods of relaxation and you should choose the one which works best for you. One popular method is to relax the muscles of the body in turn beginning first with the toes and gradually working up the body to the head, focusing particularly on the neck and shoulders. Finally focus on the stomach muscles and the breathing. After every exhale you should say the word 'relax'.This should be done 20 times. Once relaxed you should visualize your stress situation, only this time see it as a positive scene, i.e. with no stress. At the same time you should say quietly to yourself a series of positive affirmations, i.e. 'I am a confident person – I like myself and others like me – I am now able to cope with this without stress'.

This procedure should be repeated each day until complete relief is obtained.

	Yes	No	Unsure

1. I worry that I may not be able to meet deadlines.
2. I find that I often get angry with the children.
3. Nobody at work appreciates my efforts.
4. There are members of staff I do not like.
5. There are lots of children who do not like me.
6. More than one person at work dislikes me.
7. People at work often talk behind my back.
8. I wake up in the middle of the night for no reason.
9. I have trouble getting off to sleep easily.
10. I often have headaches or other pains.
11. I suffer from indigestion.
12. I have no time to read a book or a newspaper.
13. I do not take regular exercise.
14. I find I am interrupting people in conversation more than usual.
15. I find I often forget things, e.g. books, meetings, instructions.
16. I often feel like crying when discussing emotional events.
17. I am drinking more than I usually do.
18. I find I have to take work home I would normally finish at school.
19. My weight has altered noticeably during this term.
20. I find my facially muscles are tense and sometimes twitch.

Give yourself two points for all questions answering *yes* and one point for all questions answering *unsure*. Sum your score. The higher it is, the more the stress as follows:

Scores ranging from 30 to 40 = severe stress requiring professional help
Scores ranging from 20 to 30 = moderate stress: use the four-step method
Scores ranging from 5 to 20 = mild stress: take appropriate action.
Scores ranging from 0 to 5 = absence of stress

Figure 8.1 Stress questionnaire

SELF-HELP FOR STRESS

1. Face the fact that you may have to face stress situations simply because you are a teacher.
2. List possible areas of stress. You cannot cope with stress by denying it.
3. Nurture yourself by taking time out to have fun.
4. Try not keep company with people known to be miserable and unhappy.
5. Learn to say 'No' when people make too many demands on you.
6. Practise being assertive and making your needs known.
7. Delegate work where ever possible, both at home as well as in teaching.
8. Listen to your body and recognize that your energies are not limitless.
9. Take regular exercise and eat and drink in moderation
10. Learn relaxation techniques.

Further reading

Fontana, D. (1989) *Managing Stress*. BPS/Routledge, London.
Gold, Y. and Roth, R. (1993) *Teachers Managing Stress and Preventing Burnout*. Falmer, London.
Travers, C. and Cooper, C. (1995) *Teachers Under Pressure: Stress In The Teaching Profession*. Routledge, London.

Conclusion

In our western society, which is so highly competitive, teachers and parents so easily become anxious over children's attainment. They are concerned in case the children in their care should fall behind the others. The fact that children learn best when having fun is lost amongst this kind of anxiety. We need to recognize that normal development is a process of coping with the experience of failure and as teachers we need to be able to relax and enjoy the child. It is not failure which should be avoided.

Failure is an inevitable part of growing up and the first part of the process of becoming competent. It is only through trial and error that much child learning takes place. The fundamental point here is that whilst failure is an inevitable process, negative criticism need not be. It is not failure which gives concern but the way in which we adults react to failure. The ideal way to react would be to ensure first that the child was not being subjected to a situation which was totally beyond his/her level of development. It would be quite useless, for instance, to expect the normal 3-year-old to be able to cope with the game of chess. Once it has been established that learning a particular task is probably within the child's level of competence, then positive steps can be taken.

Take, for instance, the child's need to use a knife and fork properly. A first attempt is always a failure – usually with food flying in all directions. At such a time, parents are likely to become irritable, to say the least. Instead of reacting in this way, an effort should be made to come to terms with the behaviour. For example, the utensils could be rearranged so that they are within easier reach, and certainly ensuring that the child receives more practice with plenty of praise with the slightest sign of progress.

These principles apply also in the classroom. If consistently applied, the child will develop confidence to tackle new tasks without associating them with unpleasantness, and he/she is more likely to be eager to learn. This assumes, of course, that the child has received total love and acceptance from his/her parents – a topic which lies outside this book but which has an equally important part to play in the development of self-esteem.

'Learning begins in pleasure and thrives on curiosity' (Baughman, 1919). Through the enhancement of self-esteem we can achieve this and also ensure effective learning.

Further Reading

Argyle, M. (1987) *The Psychology of Happiness*. Oxford University Press, Oxford.
Dryden, W. and Gordon, J. (1994) *Think Your Way To Happiness*. Sheldon Press, London.
Rees, G. (1991) *Assertion Training*. Routledge, London.
Seligman, M. (1991) *Learned Optimism*. Random House, London.

Appendix: Investigations into self-esteem enhancement

Project – 1970

In 1970, four primary schools in Somerset, England, valiantly agreed to participate in a project designed to investigate the possibility of enhancing self-esteem among retarded readers. The four schools each submitted lists of children retarded in reading from which 12 children aged 8–9 years were matched on chronological age, sex, reading age and socioeconomic group. Each was then subjected to a different treatment.

Group 1 received remedial reading from a remedial specialist. Group 2 received remedial reading plus individual counselling to enhance self-esteem. Group 3 received counselling only, and Group 4 received ordinary class teaching. The experiment ran for 20 weeks, following which it was discovered that the 'counselling only' group (Group 3) had made the most progress not only in self-esteem enhancement but also in reading. Second came Group 2, 'remedial reading plus counselling'; third was Group 1, 'remedial reading only'; and Group 4 was last, 'ordinary class teaching' (Lawrence, 1971).

This was the first of a series of experiments by me into methods of self-esteem enhancement among primary-school children (Lawrence, 1971; 1972a; 1973; 1974; 1982; 1983; 1985).

Project – 1984

The latest experiment in the series consisted of 372 8-year-old children who were retarding in reading, and they were put into four different treatment groups.

DISTAR only – Group A

Group A received instruction in the skills of reading through the Direct Instruction in the Teaching of Arithmetic and Reading (DISTAR) technique devised by Engelmann and others (1969), published by Science Research Associates. The teachers using the method were trained for the experiment by a manager of Marketing Services (UK). She visited the teachers on four occasions before the experiment and at regular intervals during the experiment. The teaching was conducted in groups of 6–10 children, the exact number being determined by the numbers identified in each school. They received instruction three times per week for one-hour sessions. The programme continued for 20 weeks.

DISTAR plus counselling – Group B

Group B received treatment in exactly the same manner as the children in Group A. In addition they received counselling once a week for 20 weeks by non-professionals. The children were seen in pairs, each session lasting for 45 minutes. The counsellors were selected by the headteachers of the schools involved and numbered 35 altogether, working in eight different schools. They were met four times before the experiment during which they were given 'handouts' on how to structure the sessions with games and activities designed either by the author or those described by Canfield and Wells (1976). They were also briefed on self-concept theory and on the establishment of empathy as described by Rogers (1975) and 'modelling' as described by Bandura (1977). The essence of this treatment was the quality of the relationship which set out to be accepting and non-judgemental. An atmosphere of trust was established within which the children felt free to confide. The counsellors provided a confident, relaxed model. A combination of humanistic and learning theory principles were attempted.

DISTAR plus drama – Group C

The children in Group C received DISTAR remedial reading as in the two previous groups but also received a weekly drama session designed to enhance self-esteem. There were six schools involved in this treatment and groups varied in size from 7 to 15. The sessions were taken by the County Adviser for Drama and each lasted for approximately 45 minutes. The sessions were structured to allow the children to 'take risks' and experience success, as well as through role-playing of 'experts', for example, they would be on an imaginary journey and each given a different expert role. Each member had to consult with the appropriate expert before taking action. The rule was that no criticism of the expert was allowed.

Ordinary class teaching – Group D

Group D remained in the ordinary class situation receiving help as usual from their classteacher.

Once again statistically significant differences between groups were obtained with the groups receiving the counselling and the drama treatments showing most gains in self-esteem and in reading attainment. The results of this experiment showed a split in the self-esteem scores at the median point, thus analysing low self-esteem and higher self-esteem scores separately (for the full details of this experiment, see Lawrence, 1985).

References and Bibliography

Anthony, G. (1968) Cerebral dominance as an ecological factor in dyslexia, PhD dissertation, New York University.

Argyle, M. (1994) *The Psychology of Interpersonal Behaviour*, Penguin Books, Harmondsworth.

Axline, V. (1947) *Play Therapy*, Ballantine Books, New York.

Bandura, A. (1977) *Social Learning Theory*, Prentice-Hall, Englewood Cliffs, NJ.

Barker-Lunn, J.C. (1970) *Streaming in the Primary School*, NFER, Slough.

Baughman, J. (1919) *Handbook of Humor in Education*, Parker Publishing Co., West Nyack, NY.

Beker, J. (1960) The influence of school camping on the self-concepts and social relationships of sixth grade school children, *J. of Educ. Psych.*, Vol. 51, pp. 352–6.

Brophy, J. and Good, T. (1974) *Teacher–Student Relationships: Causes and Consequences*, Holt, Rinehart & Winston, New York.

Bullock. A. (ed.) (1975) *A Language of Life*, HMSO, London.

Burns, R.B. (1975) Attitudes to self and to three categories of others in a student group, *Educ. Stud.*, Vol. 1, pp. 181–9.

Burns, R.B. (1979a) The influence of various characteristics of others on social distance registered by a student group, *Irish J. Psych.*, Vol. 3, pp. 193–205.

Burns, R.B. (1979b) *The Self-Concept Theory, Measurement, Development and Behaviour*, Longman, London and New York.

Burns, R.B. (1982) *Self-Concept Development and Education*, Holt, Rinehart & Winston, Sydney.

Butler, J.M. and Haigh, G.V. (1954) Changes in the relation between self-concept and ideal concepts consequent on client-centred counselling. In Rogers and Dymond (eds.) *Psychotherapy and Personality Change*, University Press, Chicago, Ill.

Byrne, D. (1961) The repression-sensitisation scale: rationale, reliability and validity, *J. of Personality*, Vol. 29, pp. 334–49.

Canfield, J. and Wells, H. (1976) *100 Ways to Enhance Self-Concept in the Classroom*, Prentice-Hall, Englewood Cliffs, NJ.

Carkhuff, R.R. (1969) *Helping and Human Relations*, Vol. 1, Holt, Rinehart & Winston, New York.

Carkhuff, R.R. and Truax, C.B. (1967) *Towards Effective Counselling and Psychotherapy in Training and Practice*, Aldine, Chicago, Ill.

Cashdan, A. and Pumfrey, P. (1969) Some effects of the remedial teaching of reading, *Educ. Res.*, Vol. 11, no. 7, pp. 138–47.

Charles, C. (1995) *Building Classroom Discipline*, Longman, Harlow.

Chazan, M. (1967) The effects of remedial teaching in reading: a review of research, *Rem. Educ.*, Vol. 2, no. 1, pp. 4–12.

Cherniss, C. (1995) *Beyond Burnout: Helping Teachers, Nurses, Therapists and Lawyers Recover from Stress*, Routledge, London.

Collins, J.E. (1961) *The Effects of Remedial Education*, Oliver & Boyd, London.

Cooley, C.H. (1902) *Human Nature and the Social Order*, Charles Scribner's Sons, New York.

Coopersmith, S. (1967) *The Antecedents of Self-Esteem*, Freeman Press, San Francisco, Calif.

Cowie, H. and Pecherek, A. (1994) *Counselling: Approaches and Issues in Education*, Fulton, London.

De Charms, R. (1976) *Enhancing Motivation in the Classroom*, Irvington, New York.

Dryden, W. (1995) *Brief Rational/Emotive Behaviour Therapy*, Wiley, Chichester.

Ellis, A. (1979) *Theoretical and Empirical Foundations of Rational and Emotive Therapy*, Brooks/Cole, Monterey, Calif.

Englemann, S. *et al.* (1969) *DISTAR: An Instructional System*. Language I, II, III; Reading I, II, III; Arithmetic I, II, III, SRA, Chicago, Ill.

English, H.B. and English, A.C. (1958) *A Comprehensive Dictionary of Psychological and Psychoanalytical Terms*, Longman, London.

Eysenck, H. (1980) *Psychology Is About People*, Penguin Books, Harmondsworth.

116   *Enhancing Self-Esteem*

Gammage, P. (1986) *Primary Education: Structure and Context,* Paul Chapman Publishing, London.

Gordon, T. (1970) *Parent Effectiveness Training,* Peter H. Wyden, New York.

Gordon, T. (1974) *Teacher Effectiveness Training,* Peter H. Wyden, New York.

Greenhalgh, P. (1994) *Emotional Growth and Learning,* Routledge, London.

Hannum, J.W. (1974) Changing the evaluative self thoughts of two elementary teachers, *Research and Development Memorandum* No. 122, Stanford University, Calif.

Hargreaves, D. (1972) *Interpersonal Relations and Education,* Routledge, London.

James, W. (1890) *Principles of Psychology,* Vol. 1, Henry Holt, New York.

Jung, C. (1923) *Psychological Types,* Harcourt Brace, New York.

Lawrence, A. and Lawrence, D. (1996) *Self-Esteem and Your Child,* Minerva Press, London.

Lawrence, D. (1971) The effects of counselling on retarded readers, *Educ. Res.,* Vol. 13, no. 2, pp. 119–24.

Lawrence, D. (1972a) An experimental investigation into the counselling of retarded readers, unpublished MSc dissertation, University of Bristol.

Lawrence, D. (1972b) Counselling of retarded readers by nonprofessionals, *Educ. Res.,* Vol. 15, no. 1, pp. 48–54.

Lawrence, D. (1973) *Improved Reading through Counselling,* Ward Lock, London.

Lawrence, D. (1982) Development of a self-esteem questionnaire, *Br. J. Ed. Psych.,* Vol. 51, pp. 245–9.

Lawrence, D. (1983) Improving reading and self-esteem, unpublished PhD thesis, University of Western Australia.

Lawrence, D. (1985) Improving reading and self-esteem, *Educ Res.,* Vol. 27, no. 3, pp. 194–200.

Lawrence, D. and Blagg, N. (1974) Improved reading through self-initiated learning and counselling, *Rem. Ed.,* Vol. 9, no. II pp. 61–3.

Lunn, J.C.B. (1970) *Streaming in the Primary School,* NFER, Slough

Machover, K. (1949) *Personality Projection in the Drawing of the Human Figure: A Method of Personality Investigation,* Charles C Thomas, Springfield, Ill.

Marsh, H.W., Barnes, J., Cairns, L. and Tidman, M. (1984) The Self-Description Questionnaire: age effects in the structure and level of self-concept for pre-adolescent children, *J. Ed. Psych.*, Vol. 76, pp. 940–56.

Maslow, A.H. (1954) *Motivation and Personality* (2nd edn), Harper & Row, New York.

Maslow, A.H. (1962) Some basic propositions of a growth and self-actualization psychology. In A.W. Combs (ed.) *Perceiving, Behaving, Becoming*, ASCD Year Book, NEA, Washington, DC.

Murray, E. (1972) Students' perceptions of self-actualising and non self-actualising teachers, *J. of Teacher Educ.*, Vol. 23, pp. 383–7.

Omwake, K. (1954) The relation between acceptance of self and acceptance of others shown by three personality inventories, *J. Consult. Psychol.*, Vol. 18, no. 6, pp. 443–6.

Osgood, C., Suci, G. and Tannenbaum, P. (1957) *The Measurement of Meaning*, University of Illinois Press, Urbana, Ill.

Perkins, H.V. (1958) Teacher's and peers' perception of children's self-concepts, *Child Dev.*, Vol. 29, no. 2, pp. 203–20.

Piers, E.V. and Harris, D. (1969) *The Piers–Harris Children's Self-Concept Scale*, Counsellor Recordings and Tests, Nashville, Tenn.

Pratt, J. (1978) Perceived stress among teachers, *Educ. Rev.*, Vol. 30, no. 1, pp. 3–14.

Purkey, W. (1970) *Self-concept and School Achievement*, Prentice-Hall, Englewood Cliffs, NJ.

Rogers, C.R. (1951) *Client-Centered Therapy*, Houghton Mifflin, Boston, Mass.

Rogers, C.R. (1961) *On Becoming a Person*, Houghton Mifflin, Boston, Mass.

Rogers, C.R. (1967) *On Becoming a Person*, Constable, London.

Rogers, C.R. (1969) *Freedom to Learn. A View of What Education Might Become*, Merrill, Columbus, Ohio.

Rogers, C.R. (1975) Empathy: an unappreciated way of being, *The Counselling Psychologist*, Vol. 5, no. 2, pp. 2–9.

Rosenthal, R. and Jacobson, L. (1968) Self-fulfilling prophecies in the classroom: teacher expectations as unintended determinants of pupils' intellectual competence. In M. Deutsch, I. Katz and A.C. Jenson (eds.) *Social Class, Race and Psychological Development*, Holt, Rinehart & Winston, New York.

Rotter, J.B. (1954) *Social Learning and Clinical Psychology*, Prentice-Hall, Englewood Cliffs, NJ.

Rutter, M., Maughan, B., Mortimore, P. and Ouston, J. (1979) *Fifteen Thousand Hours: Secondary Schools and their Effects on Children*, Paul Chapman, London.

Schweinhart, L.J., Weikart, D.P. and Larner, M.B. (1986) Consequences of three pre-school curriculum models, *Early Child. Res. Quart.*, Vol. 1, no. 1, pp. 15–45.

Seligman, M. (1991) *Learned Optimism*, Random House, London.

Sharp, G. and Muller, D. (1978) The effects of lowering self-concept on associative learning, *J. Psych.*, Vol. 100, pp. 233–42.

Shavelson, R.J. and Bolus, R. (1982) Self-concept: the interplay of theory and methods, *J. Ed. Psych.*, Vol. 74, no. 1, pp. 3–17.

Shavelson, R.J., Hubner, J.J. and Stanton, G.G. (1976) Self-concept: validation of construct interpretations, *Rev. Ed. Res.*, Vol. 46, pp. 407–41.

Skinner, B.F. (1953) *Science and Human Behavior*, Macmillan, New York.

Smith, C.P. (ed.) (1969) *Achievement Related Motives in Children*, Russell Sage Foundation, New York.

Staines, J.W. (1958) Self picture as a factor in the classroom, *Brit. J. Psychol.*, Vol. 28, no. 2, pp. 97–111.

Stevens, R. (ed.) (1995) *Understanding the Self*, Sage, London.

Thomas, J.B. (1973) *Self-Concept in Psychology and Education*, NFER, Slough.

Thomas, J.B. (1980) *The Self in Education*, NFER, Slough.

Travers, C.J. and Cooper, C.L. (1995) *Teachers under Pressure: Stress in the Teaching Profession*, Routledge, London.

Trowbridge, N. (1973) Teacher self-concept and teaching style. In G. Chanan (ed.) *Towards a Science of Teaching*, NFER, Slough.

Wattenburg, W.W. and Clifford, C. (1964) Relation of self-concept to beginning achievement in reading, *Child Dev.*, Vol. 35, pp. 461–7.

West, C.R., Fish, J.A. and Stevens, J.A. (1980) General self-concept, self-concept of academic ability and school achievement, *Australian J. of Ed.*, Vol. 24, pp. 194–213.

Wiseman, S. (1973) The educational obstacle race: factors that hinder pupil progress, *Educ. Res.*, Vol. 15, pp. 87–93.

Wylie, R. (1974) *The Self-Concept* (2nd edn), University of Nebraska Press, Lincoln, Nebr.

Index